P9-CIS-434

DISCARD

# YOUR FUTURE WORKING WITH OLDER ADULTS

*by*

Martin Murray

Richards Rosen Press, Inc.

New York, N.Y. 10010

342.402373
M983y

To the enthusiastic young persons
employed in the field of aging,
who make every day a little better for
an older adult.

Published in 1982 by Richards Rosen Press, Inc.
29 East 21st Street, New York, N.Y. 10010

*Copyright 1982 by Martin Murray*

All rights reserved. No part of this book may be reproduced
in any form without permission in writing from
the publisher, except by a reviewer.

**First Edition**

**Library of Congress Cataloging in Publication Data**

Murray, Martin.
  Your future working with older adults
  (Careers in depth)
  1. Social work with the aged—Vocational guidance—United States.
  I. Title. II. Series.
  HV1465.M86     1982          362.6'023'73          82-9108
  ISBN 0-8239-0540-3                                 AACR2

*Manufactured in the United States of America*

# About the Author

Dr. Martin Murray, as Assistant Professor of Human Affairs at Brookdale Community College, Lincroft, New Jersey, has been involved in the field of aging since he worked as a volunteer in a nursing home in Monmouth County, New Jersey, in 1973. He has written grants and directed educational programs for older adults in community centers, senior centers, boarding homes, and nursing homes in Monmouth County. He has been a consultant on leadership training for senior leaders and for site managers at nutrition sites for the New Jersey Division on Aging. For his doctorate in education at Teachers College, Columbia University, he studied programs for older adults in community colleges in New York, Pennsylvania, and New Jersey. He served as a delegate to the Governor's Conference on Aging in New Jersey in 1981 and to the Education and Training Committee for the White House Conference on Aging in November 1981. His activities include research, observation, writing, and public advocacy for older adults. Although he has been a teacher for most of his life, his interests are varied. He has been a ranger naturalist at Grand Canyon National Park, a U.S. Marine, a paratrooper in the U.S. Army, and a camper in Iran, Afghanistan, and Pakistan.

# Contents

# Introduction

Decisions about work and career today are made extremely difficult by the rapid social and technical changes of our time, changes which make whole industries disappear in less than a generation. Yet a generation is only half the work span of many young people.

The most rapidly growing sector of our economy is the service industry—which encompasses the full range of consumer assistance, including recreational, social, legal, technical, emergency, and health services. The service industry increasingly will serve a growing elderly population. In 1900 there were 3.1 million persons above sixty-five, 4 percent of the United States population. By 1950 the number had increased to 12.4 million and by the year 2000 it is expected that there will be 32 million people over the age of sixty-five, 13 percent of the population. Given our current low birth rate and our expanded life expectancy, the baby boom of the 1940-50's will become the senior boom of the early 21st century.

The census figures show that not only will the elderly be increasing in number, but also there will be more elderly as a proportion of the total population. The number of the elderly who have some functional impairment increases from 6 percent at age sixty-five to seventy-four to 24 percent by age eighty-five and over. With increasing dependence comes increased needs in health care as well as in housing, transportation, and community social services.

It is said that the mark of a great civilization is the care that is granted to those who are most dependent. There is every sign that the United States will not forget the responsibility entailed by a large and increasingly dependent elderly population. There is opportunity for a wide variety of satisfying work in the many fields which are discussed in this book. It is important that young people are aware of those opportunities as they examine career options and plan their own educational and training programs.

I hope this book will give direction to Americans in search of a career of service.

Bill Bradley
United States Senator
New Jersey

# Chapter 1

# Why Work With Older Adults?

All of us have grandparents, and our relationship to them may influence our future career choice. Let's pose a few questions about how you think about your grandparents. For example, do you like being around them? Do you like talking with them? Are you interested in their health problems? Are you interested in their hobbies or community interests? Have you ever thought about their housing needs? You probably know that they receive some income from Social Security, but have you thought about where they obtain the money they need to live now that they no longer work? Are you concerned about what they eat? Do they seem depressed at times? While these are only general questions concerning members of your family, the answers to them may lead you to a career that involves working with senior adults.

Did you know that the number of senior adults is increasing every day? With better health care, better living conditions, and the decline in the birthrate, the percentage of senior adults in the United States population is increasing. At present senior adults represent about 11 percent of the population, or about 24 million people. About 15 million people are in the age range of sixty-five to seventy-four, about 7 million are in the age range of seventy-five to eighty-four, and 2 million are over eighty-five. These numbers will continue to increase. Planners say that by the year 2025 almost half of the U.S. population will be over fifty and senior adults will represent 22 percent of the population. Some observers have called this the "graying of America." It is sure to bring greater career opportunities for people who wish to work with senior adults.

Today, more than a million people work with senior adults in all kinds of settings. They work in senior centers, social service agencies, home health programs, nutrition projects, legal aid offices, public housing projects, retirement communities, and long-term care facilities.

The concerns of senior adults are an important aspect of government programs such as Social Security, Supplemental Security Income, veterans benefits, and Medicare. State employment offices have personnel who deal primarily with senior adults, and a growing number of community agencies have counselors who help older people get jobs. Some people plan and coordinate services for senior adults at the local, city, county, and state levels.

In other fields, educators teach courses on aging, and researchers in biology and psychology examine the causes of aging and study the aging process. Researchers also study the economic problems of senior adults and the problems of the aged among minority groups.

Perhaps in your high school studies you have had courses that deal with the aging process or describe the senior adult in our society. In many cases the description of the senior adult is unfavorable. Literature, drama, and poetry often describe the senior adult as cantankerous, stubborn, and often failing in health. Shakespeare described King Lear as being a foolish fond old man. Yet we should remember that many of our great writers, artists, and inventors have continued to work and produce as they became older. Benjamin Franklin invented bifocal glasses when he was eighty. Thomas Edison worked on many of his inventions such as the electric light bulb and the phonograph after he was sixty-five, and Pablo Picasso continued to paint until he died at the age of ninety-two. One of the goals of government offices that plan programs for senior adults is to attempt to change attitudes and beliefs about the elderly. Some observers would have us think that many elderly people are feeble or disabled in some way that keeps them from participating in community life. Actually, these observers are wrong. Only 5 percent of senior adults live in nursing homes, and over 80 percent of all senior adults live in their own homes. Today the Gray Panthers and other leadership groups working with senior adults are attempting to change the image of senior adults that is portrayed on television, on radio, and in movies. Some current television programs dealing with the life-style of senior adults show them playing tennis, camping, swimming, dancing, and participating in many other athletic activities. The television program "Over Easy" with Hugh Downs is an example of programs that attempt to describe the activities of senior adults throughout the United States.

These activities are growing in number and scope in every community as a result of the passage of the Older Americans Act of 1965. But the growth is not simply because the passage of a law led to an increase in government programs for senior adults. It is because of the increased number of older adults who are participating in all types of activities and programs in communities, cities, and towns throughout the United States.

If you decide to work with older adults, what special attitudes or skills do you need? You must first realize the disadvantages of working with older adults. You will not be working with young people, with whom you can often see success almost immediately. With senior adults this will not be true. You will find that everything will take longer and that you will need patience in your work. Another obvious disadvantage is that senior adults with whom you become friendly either on the job or through recreational activities are more likely to become ill or disabled or die than young people.

At first the problems that you will confront and that senior adults describe to you may seem very large. You must not let their problems overwhelm you. You will need to identify the most important problem of a senior adult and attempt to deal with that problem. You should remember that the persons you are working with have lived sixty, seventy, or eighty years without any help from you and that most of them are two and a half to three times older than you. You may also find that senior adults love to talk about their problems and describe them in such graphic detail that you want to take immediate action. However, you must remember that the senior adult has been coping with these problems. You must avoid jumping to conclusions, but rather be objective in dealing with senior adults. In some cases you will find that the agency you work for cannot do anything about a particular problem. In other cases you will find that your agency or organization is equipped to deal with specific problems affecting senior adults. You may also follow referral techniques by taking down information on an individual senior adult and then referring him or her to a community agency that can provide the services needed.

It will help you to know something about the science of gerontology. Webster's dictionary defines gerontology as the branch of knowledge that deals with the aged and the problems of the aged. Courses and programs of study are offered in this subject that will help you in understanding the senior adult by being aware of the biological, psychological, and sociological changes that occur during the later years of life.

Certain specific attitudes will be helpful to you in working with senior adults. You will be entering a service-oriented or helping profession. You will in effect be a service provider. You should think carefully about this, because you will not be entering a production-oriented industry. In many instances you will work in a nonprofit or government agency whose main objective is helping people.

The attitudes needed for success in any career situation are also needed when working with senior adults. You should be a caring and a compassionate person with a positive attitude toward the problems and situations that you meet. At first, you may not be certain that you are equipped to work with senior adults, and you may find out very quickly that the field is not for you. You may find that you do not have the patience or that you become easily depressed.

Just as your friends differ from one another, you will find that no two senior adults are identical in manner or appearance. Yet you must try to understand and like the individuals that you meet in your work. Many of the personality characteristics that you find in your friends will also exist in senior adults. Some will be happy and outgoing while others will be angry and bitter toward the world in general and you in particular.

Many of the personality traits that you will need in working with senior adults are required to succeed in any job or life situation, and that includes school, part-time work, recreation, or community activities. You will need to be creative, have a sense of humor, and like what you are doing. Senior adults are a product of all their experiences, and you can learn from them. But in order to learn you must develop your ability to listen. Because of the broad range of experiences and interests that you will meet with, you will find yourself always learning—learning more about senior adults and more about your job.

When considering any field or vocation, one wants to know the opportunities for advancement. In the field of working with senior adults, there are pluses and minuses. Many jobs in this field are relatively new and low-paying. By entering the vocation when you are young and obtaining on-the-job experience and further schooling, you can make contacts and learn about other job opportunities. The executive positions in planning and management, however, pay as well as any other line of work that you might select. Your opportunities for advancement in the field of aging will come about through your own creativeness and willingness to work.

Experience in this field can be obtained in many ways: through volunteer work, work-study programs in high school, community project activities, and as a member of a service organization such as Explorer Scout groups. You can also obtain summer jobs while in high school or college that put you in contact with senior adults before making your decision to enter the field. Internship and field placement courses in college can help you round out your experience.

If you wish to work for a government agency, you will be required to pass a civil service examination for the position you desire. You may also be required to obtain a state license if your position requires it. Civil Service positions may be at the local, city, state, or Federal level. It will be up to you to start at the entrance level and make the most of your opportunities.

Opportunities can be found throughout the United States. You will find a greater number of programs and activities for senior adults in cities and larger states than in towns and smaller states; however, programs and services for senior adults are being created and expanded throughout the country. Certain states have large concentrations of senior adults, among them Florida, Maryland, Virginia, New York, Massachusetts, Pennsylvania, Illinois, Texas, and California. You will also find areas in your own state having large concentrations of senior adults. More jobs should be available in those areas, and you should be able to find the opportunity and position that you desire.

What type of facility will you be working in? That will depend on whether you elect to work with the healthy senior adult, the frail senior adult, or the institutionalized senior adult. The major portion of the jobs discussed in this book will be in services and programs in the aging network. This network was created through passage of the Older Americans Act of 1965, which was designed to help senior adults maintain their health and independence. It attempts to focus on the characteristics, needs, and resources of older people, and it includes programs for nutrition and employment. It emphasizes the need for health care and social services particularly for the frail senior adult. The facilities related to the fulfillment of these needs will be the source of many jobs in future years.

The facilities that exist and are being created for senior adults are sometimes called community focal points. They include an Area Agency on Aging in almost every county in the country. These agencies sponsor programs for the healthy, the frail, and the institutionalized elderly. As their programs and services increase, the number of staff required also increases. The community focal points where programs and services for senior adults are provided include the community nutrition site, the senior center, the adult day-care center, the boarding home, nursing or convalescent home, and the hospice. In addition, various types of housing facilities for senior adults are being constructed or have been built. Each of these focal points will be described in detail.

Many high school students want to enter the teaching field. Although the demand for elementary and secondary teachers is decreasing as the number of students declines, this is not true of demand for education by senior adults. That demand is expected to expand in coming years. Therefore, opportunities for teaching senior adults will be identified and described. These opportunities for teaching will arise in senior centers, community nutrition sites, day-care centers, boarding homes, and nursing homes. A small percentage of senior adults will continue their education in community colleges and major universities. Some instructors will find that their classes include a large number of senior adults ready and willing to learn. Knowledge of gerontology and ability to work with senior adults will aid the student who desires to major in education and teach this age group.

There are many national organizations that work with older adults. These organizations sponsor programs and services related to their goals. You will learn about these organizations and how their growth provides new opportunities for young persons entering the job market.

The aim of this book is to give the reader an idea of what these positions are, what the requirements are for employment, and what skills are needed to work with senior adults. If you decide to enter this field and you are able to provide some service that brings a smile to the face of a senior adult or a thank you for a job well done, then you will have succeeded in your chosen vocation. You will also find that most jobs in this field will bring a sense of satisfaction to you as you go about your daily work and at the completion of your career.

# Chapter II

# Education and Training Requirements

What should be your training and education if you wish to succeed in the field of aging? Adam Smith, the famous Scottish economist, once said that most people go into a vocation for two reasons: one for their own self-interest, and the other to satisfy the needs of society. You will read in this book about many young persons who are satisfying their self-interest and at the same time fulfilling the needs of society.

Before you decide on a specific career in the field of aging, you should find out what kinds of jobs exist. You can do this by visiting your local college or Area Agency on Aging or a senior center close to your home. When you know the opportunities that are available, you should make a choice to meet your own vocational interests. If you are returning to school, it would be advisable to analyze yourself. In almost every county there is a community college or state college where you can take a battery of tests to determine your interests or aptitudes as compared with successful people in a particular field.

To work in the field of aging, you should have an aptitude for human service. The two most important aspects of your background will be your education and your experience or training. In most cases, you will be hired on the basis of these factors. Once hired, you will receive on-the-job training.

Many new professionals in the field of aging have no previous experience with older people. Others have obtained experience through volunteer work, cooperative work-study programs, and

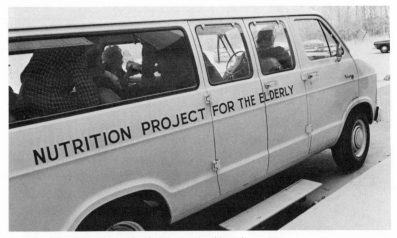

Older adults are transported to lunch at a nutrition site.

internship. Still others have prepared themselves by studying geron-tology. The study of aging, gerontology consists of several disciplines including biology and physiology, which investigate physical aging, or the gradual decline of bodily strength and func-tion; psychology, which studies emotional stability and the self-concept and personality through which people express themselves as they are; and sociolpgy, which studies roles and responsibilities in situations where older persons interact with others in the family, education, religion, occupation, leisure, and the community.

## TRAINING IN GERONTOLOGY

Many colleges and universities have developed two-year associate, four-year bachelor's, and five- and six-year master's degree programs in gerontology. Some institutions of higher educa-tion offer a PhD degree in gerontology and related disciplines. One of your best opportunities to begin your career education is the local community college that offers courses in social science and human service skills that can be used with older adults. Often you can train as a paraprofessional and after two years of study enter the field of aging. Later you can transfer these credits to a four-year college program and take further courses in the vocational area that you have chosen.

A pickup schedule is arranged for a transportation service.

The Ethel Percy Andrus Gerontology Center at the University of Southern California is an example of an institution offering graduate and undergraduate programs in gerontology. In the undergraduate school a bachelor of science degree in gerontology is offered, and an undergraduate certificate in gerontology is awarded to students who are working toward a bachelor's degree in another discipline. At the graduate level, a master of science in gerontology is offered with four specialization areas: direct service, administration, health services, and industrial gerontology. Master's level training involves an integrated course of study in gerontology and sometimes the completion of a thesis on a topic in the field of aging. This typically requires two years of work beyond the bachelor's degree. Most graduate and many undergraduate programs require an internship or field placement in addition to required coursework.

*TWO-YEAR COLLEGES OFFERING*
*GERONTOLOGY COURSES*

The two-year colleges listed below offer courses in gerontology or concentrations in gerontology. In some instances, an associate in arts degree with a concentration in gerontology is offered.

Alexander City State Community College, Alexander City, AL
Allegheny County, Community College of, Pittsburgh, PA
Baltimore, Community College of, Baltimore, MD
Broward Community College, Fort Lauderdale, FL
Catonsville Community College, Catonsville, MD
Chicago Citywide College, Chicago, IL
Delta College, University Center, MI
Elgin Community College, Elgin, IL
Grand Rapids Junior College, Grand Rapids, MI
Harford Community College, Bel Air, MD
Lake County, College of, Grayslake, IL
Laney Community College, Oakland, CA
Lansing Community College, Lansing, MI
Manhattan Community College, New York, NY
Middlesex Community College, Bedford, MA
Minneapolis Community College, Minneapolis, MN
Minnesota, University of, Technical Institute, Crookston, MN
Misericordia, College of, Dallas, PA
Molloy College, Rockville Centre, NY
Charles Stewart Mott College, Flint, MI
Mount St. Mary's College, Emmitsburg, MD
Nebraska, University of, Medical Center, Omaha, NE
New York at Stony Brook, State University of, Stony Brook, NY
New York at Utica/Rome, State University of, Utica, NY
New York City Community College, New York, NY
New York College at New Paltz, St. University of, New Paltz, NY
Niagara University, Niagara Falls, NY
Norfolk State College, Norfolk, VA
North Country Community College, Saranac Lake, NY
Northeast Louisiana University, Monroe, LA
Northern Kentucky University, Highland Heights, KY
Oakland University, Rochester, MI

Ocean County Community College, Toms River, NJ
Ohio State University, Columbus, OH
Oregon, University of, Eugene, OR
Oregon State University, Corvallis, OR
Palm Beach Junior College, Lake Worth, FL
Palomar Community College, San Marcos, CA
Paris Junior College, Paris, TX
Paul Quinn College, Waco, TX
Portland State University, Portland, OR
Puerto Rico, University of, Rio Piedras, PR
Ramapo College of New Jersey, Mahwah, NJ
Rhode Island College, Providence, RI
Riverside City College, Riverside, CA
Rockland Community College, Suffern, NY
Saddleback Community College, Mission Viejo, CA
Saint John Fisher College, Rochester, NY
Saint Scholastica, College of, Duluth, MN
Saint Thomas Aquinas College, Santa Paula, CA
Santa Clara, University of, Santa Clara, CA
Scranton, University of, Scranton, PA
Seminole College, Sanford, FL
Slippery Rock State College, Slippery Rock, PA
Southeastern Massachusetts University, North Dartmouth, PA
Southern Idaho, College of, Twin Falls, ID
Southern University in New Orleans, LA
South Oklahoma City Junior College, Oklahoma City, OK
Stockton State College, Pomona, NJ
Texas, University of, Health Center, Dallas, TX
Union College, Cranford, NJ
Utica College, Utica, NY
Virginia Union University, Richmond, VA
Vista Community College, CA
Wayne Community College, Goldsboro, NC
Weber State College, Ogden, UT
Webster College, St. Louis, MO

Western Illinois University, Macomb, IL
Western Michigan University, Kalamazoo, MI
William Paterson College, Wayne, NJ
Winthrop College, Rock Hill, SC
Wisconsin State University–Stevens Point, WI
Wisconsin–Green Bay, University of, Green Bay, WI
York College of Pennsylvania, York, PA

Below is a list of members of the Association for Gerontology in Higher Education that offer four-year gerontology programs on the undergraduate level.

*Four-year Gerontology Programs*
Appalachian State University, Boone, NC
Arizona State University, Tempe, AZ
Arkansas–Pine Bluff, University of, AR
Baldwin-Wallace College, Berea, OH
Baltimore, University of, Baltimore, MD
Bethune-Cookman College, Daytona Beach, FL
Bowling Green State University, Bowling Green, OH
Bridgeport, University of, Bridgeport, CT
British Columbia, University of, Vancouver, Canada
California State College of Pennsylvania, California, PA
California State College, Stanislaus, CA
California State University, Chico, CA
Calumet College, Whiting, IN
Canisius College, Buffalo, NY
Capital University, Columbus, OH
Central Washington University, Ellensburg, OH
Cincinnati, University of, Cincinnati, OH
Cleveland State University, Cleveland, OH
Colorado State University, Fort Collins, CO
Columbia University, New York, NY
Delaware, University of, Newark, DE
District of Columbia, University of the, Washington, DC

East Carolina University, Greenville, NC
East Central Oklahoma University, Ada, OK
Eastern Michigan University, Ypsilanti, MI
Edinboro State College, Edinboro, PA
Elmira College, Elmira, NY
Ferrum College, Ferrum, VA
Gannon University, Erie, PA
Gwynedd–Mercy College, Gwynedd Valley, PA
Hamline University, St. Paul, MN
Hampton Institute, Hampton, VA
Hood College, Frederick, MD
Hunter College of the City of New York, NY
Iona College, New Rochelle, NY
Jacksonville State University, Jacksonville, AL
Jersey City State College, Jersey City, NJ
Kean College, Union, NJ
Kent State University, Kent, OH
Kentucky, University of, Lexington, KY
Kentucky State University, Frankfort, KY
Mankato State University, Mankato, MN
Marion College, Marion, IN
Medgar Evers College of the City of New York, NY
Mercy College of Detroit, Detroit, MI
Nebraska Medical Center, Omaha, NE
Norfolk State College, Norfolk, VA
Northeast Louisiana University, Monroe, LA
Northern Kentucky University, Highlands Heights, KY
Oakland University, Rochester, MI
Ohio State University, Columbus, OH
Oregon State University, Corvallis, OR
Unversity of Oregon, Eugene, OR
William Patterson College, Wayne, NJ
Portland State University, Portland, OR
University of Puerto Rico, Rio Piedras, PR
Paul Quinn College, Waco, TX

Ramapo College, Mahwah, NJ
Rhode Island College, Providence, RI
College of Saint Elizabeth, Convent Station, NJ
St. John Fisher College, Rochester, NY
College of St. Scholastica, Duluth, MN
St. Thomas Aquinas College, Sparkill, NY
University of Santa Clara, Santa Clara, CA
Slippery Rock State College, Slippery Rock, PA
Southeastern Massachusetts University, North Dartmouth, MA
Southern University in New Orleans, LA
Stockton State College, Pomona, NJ
University of Scranton, Scranton, PA
State University of New York-New Paltz, NY
State University of New York-Stony Brook, NY
State University of New York-Utica/Rome, Utica, NY
Southwestern Missouri State University, Springfield, MO
Virginia Union University, Richmond, VA
Weber State College, Ogden, UT
Webster College, St. Louis, MO
Western Illinois University, Macomb, IL
Western Michigan University, Kalamazoo, MI
Winthrop College, Rockhill, SC
York College of Pennsylvania, York, PA
Utica College, Utica, NY
University of Wisconsin-Green Bay, Green Bay, WI

## *EDUCATIONAL TRAINING OF STAFF PERSONNEL IN AGING FIELD*

What seems to be the educational background of the professionals who have been interviewed for this book? Perhaps the commonest degree for the entry-level college graduate in the field of aging is in social science. With a BA in psychology or sociology, the student has had some opportunity to participate in field work or internships in the field of aging.

On the MA level, the degree that a large number of staff personnel have received is the master of social work or MSW degree. The field of social work is concerned with the investigation, treatment, and material aid of the economically underprivileged and socially maladjusted. Today the social worker is also involved in community organization and community planning and in advocacy for various groups within the community.

## SOURCES OF INFORMATION ON CAREERS IN AGING

Listed below are sources of information on careers in aging. In most cases, education, training, and licensing procedures are mentioned. It should be pointed out that the professions listed serve the entire population, but many of them are beginning to specialize in treating older adults.

### Nurses

Programs in nursing are offered in almost every college and university throughout the country. The requirements vary from one year of training for a licensed practical nurse (LPN) to four years for a bachelor's degree in nursing. Many community colleges offer two-year programs for the registered nurse (RN) certificate. Many hospitals offer two- and three-year programs in nursing education. Consult your local community college or hospital to determine their requirements in this field.

### Gerontological Nurse

Gerontological nursing is concerned with the health needs of older adults, planning and implementing health care to meet those needs, and evaluating the effectiveness of such care. The American Nurses' Association grants certification as a gerontological nurse if you meet these requirements:

1. Have two years of practice as a gerontological nurse immediately prior to application.

2. Submit evidence of continuing education relevant to gerontological nursing during the previous two years.
3. Receive a passing score in the examination for certification.

The examination for gerontological nurse covers attitudes toward the aging process, influences of the aging process, health and health care needs of older adults, factors that affect the health and health care of older adults, and issues that affect gerontological nursing practice.

*Gerontological Nurse Practitioner*

A gerontological nurse practitioner is a registered nurse who has received specialized education as preparation for delivering primary health care services to older adults. There are two avenues for preparation as a nurse practitioner: continuing education programs provided by an accredited school or department of nursing within an institution of higher education, and master's degree programs. Persons who have successfully completed such programs in gerontological nursing may use the title Gerontological Nurse Practitioner.

The requirements include:

1. Submission of transcript and a letter from the dean or director of your baccalaureate or master's degree program certifying that the program meets specific guidelines.
2. Passing of a written test in gerontological nursing. The test includes patient assessment, interpretation and management of patient information, and evaluation of patient care.

For further information concerning certification write to:

Division on Gerontological Nursing Practice
American Nurses' Association
2420 Pershing Road
Kansas City, MO 64108

## Social Work

The National Association of Social Workers accredits social workers on the bachelor's and master's degree levels. Programs in social work are offered in most colleges and universities throughout the United States. If you are interested, contact the nearest college or university in your state, or write to:

National Association of Social Workers
1425 H Street, NW
Washington, DC 20005

## Occupational Therapist

The registered occupational therapist (OTR) has completed a four-year bachelor's degree program and six to nine months of field work experience. The OTR may have spent the full four years in an occupational therapy program or may have transferred to occupational therapy after two years in a liberal arts program. Coursework includes physical, biological, and behavioral sciences and is followed by supervised field work dealing with conditions commonly met in practice. After successful completion of all requirements, it is necessary to pass a national certification examination to become an OTR. There are more than 50 programs throughout the United States leading to this qualification.

For the person who already has a bachelor's degree in an area other than occupational therapy, entry-level master's degree programs are available. Some schools may require post-bachelor students to have credits in human growth and development, psychology, sociology, or anthropology. The master's degree program usually requires 45 semester credits plus six to nine months of field work.

There is also a certified occupational therapy assistant (COTA) program. COTAs are high school graduates or the equivalent who complete an associate degree program in an accredited university or junior community college, or a one-year certificate program in an accredited educational institution. Graduates are eligible for certification upon passage of a national certification examination. At present there are about 45 of these programs in colleges and universities throughout the country.

Career opportunities exist in hospitals, clinics, rehabilitation centers, home-care programs, community health centers, nursing homes, day-care centers, and psychiatric facilities.

For information concerning occupational therapy programs, consult your state university or community college. For further information write to:

Public Affairs Division
American Occupational Therapy Association, Inc.
6000 Executive Boulevard, Suite 200
Rockville, MD 20852

*Physical Therapist*
The goals of the American Physical Therapist Association include the development and improvement of physical therapy education, practice, and research in order to meet the physical needs of all adults. If you are considering a career in physical therapy, you should begin taking courses in the physical and biological sciences while in high school. The educational programs for physical therapists are similar to those for premedical students. All programs include general education requirements, basic science courses, and emphasis on the theory and practice of physical therapy.

You should become familiar with the requirements at your state university or school of allied health professions. Most offer a bachelor's degree course or 120 credit hours leading to a degree in physical therapy. Other schools have a certificate program for college graduates of 12 to 16 months' duration. Some schools have a master's degree program. Most master's programs do not require an undergraduate degree in physical therapy, but you should check with your college or university to determine the exact requirements. At the master's level your program will include basic health sciences, clinical sciences, and supervised clinical experience.

*Licensure or Registration*

The practice of physical therapy is regulated by state law in all fifty states, the District of Columbia, and the Commonwealth of Puerto Rico. Licensure means the legal right to practice. State examinations are given once a year, and physical therapists must comply with the legal requirements of the state in which they practice.

*Physical Therapist Assistant*

The physical therapist assistant normally works under the supervision of a physical therapist. The duties of a physical therapist assistant include training patients in activities for daily living, assisting patients to use specialized equipment, and testing and evaluating patient responses.

The majority of physical therapist assistant programs are given in community and junior colleges and are two years in length. The course of study includes physical, biological, and social sciences, physical therapy technical courses, and clinical experience. Graduates receive an associate degree as physical therapist assistant.

*Physical Therapy Aide*

If you are eighteen or older and have not decided on your career goals, you might consider becoming a physical therapy aide. You will be expected to complete an on-the-job training program in a hospital or other clinical facility. Your primary function will be to perform routine tasks related to the operation of a physical therapy program. You will work with the physical therapist or physical therapist assistant and assist in patient-related activities. If you are interested in becoming a physical therapy aide, contact the chief physical therapist or the personnel director of your local hospital or clinic.

To find out more about physical therapy, visit a physical therapy department in your local hospital or clinic, talk with your guidance counselor, or write to specific educational programs concerned with physical therapy in your state. You might also contact:

American Physical Therapy Association
1156 15th Street, NW
Washington, DC 20005

*Recreation Therapist*

The recreation therapist is employed in nursing homes, hospitals, Veterans Administration facilities, mental institutions, and National Park facilities. In each case the recreation therapist is involved in developing programs and leading patient activities. Various levels of registration standards have been adopted by the National Therapeutic Recreation Society. These range from on-the-job training for a therapeutic recreation assistant to an associate degree for a therapeutic recreation technician level II. A therapeutic recreation leader is expected to have a bachelor's degree from an accredited college or university with a major in therapeutic recreation. A therapeutic recreation specialist would be required to have either a master's degree with a major in therapeutic recreation or a bachelor's degree with appropriate experience.

Aside from opportunities in private nonprofit facilities, many positions are advertised each year in civil service bulletins of city and state employment offices. Contact the state civil service commission in your state for information on openings in the therapeutic recreation field. The National Park Service in Washington, DC, is developing a Special Program and Populations division in which qualified therapeutic recreation specialists will be employed. County and city park departments are beginning to hire therapeutic recreational specialists to offer programs for special populations including older adults. For further information write to:

National Recreation and Park Association
1601 North Kent Street
Arlington, VA 22209

*Art Therapist*

A number of colleges and universities offer training in art therapy. Most state colleges and universities have programs on the undergraduate level. Institutions that offer graduate training in art therapy include: California State University, Sacramento, CA; George Washington University, Washington, DC; Hahneman

Medical College, Philadelphia, PA; Temple University, Philadelphia, PA; Godddard College, Plainfield, VT; University of Houston at Clear Lake City, TX; University of Louisville, Louisville, KY; New York University, New York, NY; and Pratt Institute, Brooklyn, NY.

The training for an art therapist includes both theory and practice with various age groups. Usually in the second year of coursework, the student elects to specialize in a particular area and is expected to write a thesis.

In some graduate programs, the student is expected to have some knowledge of art therapy, movement therapy, and music therapy and to have in-depth training in one of these disciplines. For further information concerning art therapy education, write to:

American Art Therapy Association
P.O. Box 11602
Pittsburgh, PA.

*Dance or Movement Therapy*

Dance therapists work with persons who have social, emotional, or physical problems. They are employed in psychiatric hospitals, clinics, community mental health centers, and special schools and agencies. Dance therapy is the use of movement to improve personality and physical coordination.

A liberal arts background with emphasis in psychology is recommended. Extensive training in a variety of dance forms is suggested, with experience in teaching dance to normal children and adults. Survey courses in dance therapy can help students determine their interests and aptitudes before entering a graduate program. Master's degree programs in dance or movement therapy can be found throughout the United States. Many programs are two years in duration and include a variety of psychological approaches. Most programs include an internship or supervised field work with different types of individuals. If you were interested in working with older adults, you would be expected to specialize in movement therapy for that age group. For further information concerning dance therapy, write to:

American Dance Therapy Association
2000 Century Plaza
Columbia, MD 21044

*Nursing Home Administrator*

All states require licensure of administrators practicing within their boundaries. All states require passage of a formal test. The large majority of states require formal education ranging from a high school diploma through an associate to a bachelor's degree. A majority of states require a six- to twelve-month Administrator in Training residency in a licensed nursing home. Some states require a certain amount of formal education in nursing home or health services administration. In the future more and more candidates are expected to have a master's degree in nursing home administration. Organizations that deal with long-term care include:

American College of Nursing Home Administrators
4560 East-West Highway
Washington, DC 20014

American Health Care Association
1200 15th Street, NW
Washington, DC 20005

American Association of Homes for the Aging
374 National Press Building
41st and F Streets, NW
Washington, DC

You can join the College of Nursing Home Administrators as a student affiliate. You can also obtain from the college a pamphlet entitled "State Licensure Requirements," which will provide you with up-to-date information for your state.

*Librarian, Gerontology Specialization*

These schools provide specialization for librarians wishing to serve older adults:

Wayne State University
College of Education
Division of Library Science
Detroit, MI 48202

Rutgers University
Graduate School of Library Science
4 Huntington Lane
New Brunswick, NJ 08903

*Dietitian*

The qualifications for dietitian include a BS degree in foods and nutrition with a coordinated undergraduate program that includes an internship or traineeship. Dietitians are hired to work in hospitals, homes for the elderly, nursing homes, and various government facilities including veterans' hospitals. Dietitians with advanced degrees in dietetics are in demand for teaching and research positions in medical centers, colleges, and universities.

Many dietitians belong to the American Dietetic Association. This organization accredits and approves college and university programs for dietitians, dietetic assistants, and dietetic technicians in the United States. There are coordinated undergraduate programs for dietitians in more than thirty-five states. To become an active member of the American Dietetic Association, the student must complete a post-bachelor's internship, usually six to twelve months in duration. Many of these internships offer graduate credit or a master's degree.

*Dietetic Technician*

The preparation for dietetic technician is usually a two-year program leading to dietetic work under the supervision of a dietitian. Accredited dietetic technician programs are found throughout the country in community colleges and vocational technical schools.

For further information concerning accredited dietetic programs, write to:

American Dietetic Association
430 North Michigan Avenue
Chicago, IL 60611

The Hospital, Institution, and Educational Food Service Society was established for the purpose of maintaining a high level of quality in dietary departments of related health care facilities such as nursing homes, hospitals, and school lunch programs as well as establishments where groups of people are fed. Many programs are offered in accredited junior colleges, community colleges, vocational and adult education schools, and through correspondence courses in food service management and in nutrition care.

The two main occupational titles in the Society's program are:

*Dietetic assistant:* one who is responsible for providing food service supervision and nutritional care services under the supervision of a dietetian, a dietetic technician, or an administrator. A certified dietetic assistant has completed sucessfully a one-year program that has been approved by the Society.

*Dietetic technician:* a person who has an associate degree in food service and nutrition from a program approved by the Society. The dietetic technician works under the supervision of a dietitian. He or she assists in food service management or in providing nutritional care services under the supervision of a dietitian or an administrator. With experience, leadership, and a background in food service administration and nutrition care, the opportunities for promotion are excellent. New positions are being created every day. It is estimated that there is a need for ten times the present number of dietetic assistants and dietetic technicians.

For further information, write to:
Hospital, Institution, and Educational Food Service Society
4410 West Roosevelt Road
Hillside, IL 60162

*Public Housing Manager*

The National Association of Housing and Redevelopment Officials is an organization that works with local, state, Federal, and private agencies to provide decent living arrangements for all Americans. The organization provides testing and certification for public housing managers. The required experience is that acquired by one who performs or supervises the tasks associated with the operation of low-rent housing developments or projects owned or administered by public housing agencies. There are at present two ways in which a person may be certified as a manager of public housing: (1) four years of experience as a manager of public housing; and (2) test and candidate review for public housing manager.

The Housing Manager certification test is given at colleges in every state of the U.S. during the third week of each month. The test consists of two parts. One is a multiple-choice test in five general areas: maintenance, resident services, occupancy cycle, management, and administration. The second part is a candidate review exercise in which you assume the role of a newly hired public housing manager in a representative setting and are expected to make decisions about problems and case studies that are given to you.

For information concerning the examination, write to:

Housing Manager Certification Program
National Association of Housing and Redevelopment Officials
2600 Virginia Avenue, Suite 404
Washington, DC 20037

*Hospice Programs*

Teamwork is important in hospice programs. Therefore you

should possess various skills. At present nursing and social work are very marketable skills. However, a master's degree in nursing, public health, or health care administration would make one better qualified for a position in hospices. Experience in fiscal management, fund raising, and supervisory or administrative work is often required. Experience as a community health nurse or clinical nurse specialist is helpful. At present, two hospices offer postgraduate training, although they are nondegree courses:

Hospice of Marin
77 Mark Drive #6
San Rafael, CA 94903

Hospice of Connecticut, Inc.
61 Burban Drive
Branford, CT 06405

Many community colleges are beginning to offer short courses concerned with the development and operation of a hospice program.

### Medical Records Technician

The purpose of the medical records technology program is to provide trained graduates to serve as medical records technicians in hospitals, nursing homes, health maintenance organizations, insurance companies, and other health care organizations throughout the United States.

The program consists of a combination of general education, medical records and medical records-related courses taken during a two-year span. Courses include human anatomy and physiology, community health, human relations, medical terminology, and medical record science courses. Courses are given in almost every state, usually in community colleges or technical colleges. Upon completion of the associate degree program, the student is expected to pass an examination provided by the American Medical Record Association.

*Medical Records Administration*

The medical records administrator supervises the acquisition of complete medical records on each patient cared for by the medical team, plans record-keeping and methods of record retrieval, and supervises maintenance of patient records. The medical record is used to aid the medical team in the treatment and diagnosis of the patient's illness, to verify insurance claims, and to provide a source of legal information. The Medical Records Administration program requires coursework in physical sciences, mathematics, English, and foreign languages in addition to medical records administration courses.

In order to qualify for the title of Medical Records Administrator (MRA), the student must be a graduate of a program for medical records administrators approved by the designated accrediting authority. Currently these are four-year programs that lead to a BS degree. Many programs are two years in length with two years of previous college credit required. Programs in Medical Records Administration are offered in over thirty-five states. Upon completion of the degree program, the student is expected to pass an examination provided by the American Medical Records Association.

For further information write to:

American Medical Records Association
875 North Michigan Avenue
Chicago, IL 60611

*In-Service or On-the-Job Training*

If you become employed in the aging field, your Area Agency on Aging or State Agency on Aging may receive Federal funds usually connected with Title IV-A of the Older Americans Act. Although the amount and extent of these grants vary from state to state, they are usually given to people in the aging network who are employed by area or state agencies on aging. Grants are provided to colleges and universities for gerontology programs. Grants are also provided for in-service training, direct training, and tuition for courses that are related to the employee's job responsibilities.

# Chapter III

# Area Office on Aging

Where will you find opportunities to work with older adults? Perhaps the most important agency that deals with older adults in every county and state of the U.S. is the Area Office on Aging. There are over 600 Area Offices on Aging in the country, and twelve cities have been designated Area Offices on Aging. It is through these offices that the Federal government distributes funds for programs for older adults. In addition, the director of the Area Office on Aging is in charge of monitoring local programs that receive funds from the Area Office in each county.

There are also job opportunities at the Area Office on Aging. In each office there is a director, an information and referral specialist, a supervisor of outreach workers, a director or coordinator of home health services, and various planners and program directors who are employed to carry out office functions depending on the size and scope of the office. A rural area agency on aging may have only one or more of these positions. A larger office may have a large number of planners, program specialists, and information and referral specialists to handle the larger population of older adults in the immediate area.

The Area Office monitors and coordinates many kinds of programs and services. These include programs in transportation, home service, congregate nutrition, senior centers, outreach, and health screening. Most of these jobs require training, experience, or education in the field of aging. Your background may help you qualify for a job with one of the agencies that are responsible for carrying out a particular function or program connected with serving older adults in your community.

In New Jersey a legal service corporation has been set up to help older adults with legal problems. Funds for this program are provided by an Area Office on Aging. Carol Rogers and Jean Erickson (not their real names) are the two lawyers involved in providing legal assistance for older adults. Their job is not glamorous, nor do they earn the salary of a Wall Street lawyer, but they attempt to provide free legal assistance for as many older adults as possible.

Many of the cases that Carol and Jean handle deal with consumer problems. Many cases deal with older adults who are having difficulty obtaining benefits from Federal or state agencies. Carol and Jean also provide advice on wills and estate problems. As director of the Legal Services center, Carol is involved in training paralegals — assistants who work under the supervision of a lawyer in a senior center, nutrition site, or other community center.

Jean points out that in order to help older adults you have to know whom to call or write. If you decide to work in legal assistance for the elderly, you will need to be familiar with the aging network, that is, what agencies work with older adults. You will also need to know how to perform information and referral services for older adults; in cases where you are unable to help, you will have to determine what agency can help them.

Both Carol and Jean find their jobs rewarding. Legal assistance for the elderly is a new field and a growing one in which they find plenty of opportunities to utilize their knowledge of the law. What kind of legal problems does the older adult bring to their office? There are problems connected with Social Security and supplemental security benefits, problems with pensions and with former employers of the older adult. There are problems with nursing homes involving the rights of patients with which older adults may not be familiar. Older adults may need advice on handling the estate of a deceased spouse or relative. Perhaps the older adult wants to insure that someone be given power to handle his or her affairs in the event of illness or disability. Perhaps he or she is having difficulty getting an apartment in a senior citizen housing complex or having a problem with the manager of an apartment or housing complex. Perhaps he or she belong to a club or organization that wants to incorporate. All of these situations are legal problems that the Legal Services center tries to handle.

Almost every Area Office on Aging coordinates or supervises some type of transportation program for older adults. Because transportation service for older adults is often poor, bus or van transportation has been developed in many communities to take older adults to the doctor, to visit government agencies, or to go shopping.

Sometimes medical transportation is a matter of life or death. Margaret Salese is Assistant Director of the Ocean County Handicapped Elderly Transportation Service in Toms River, New Jersey. The OCHETS transports handicapped or very ill older adults to hospitals for outpatient medical services, including cancer treatment or kidney dialysis. When asked what sort of person you should be to do a job like this, Margaret said, "You must be a caring person because you often work long hours for little pay. Every day you deal with death and dying. You must be very human relations-oriented. It is not enough to know vehicle maintenance. You get to know the older adults that you transport. They discuss problems with you and they become very special to you and the drivers that transport them week in and week out."

What education and training does Marge have to be assistant director of a medical transportation program? Marge started in 1971-72 as a first-aid squad member in Pleasant Plains, New Jersey. In eight years of voluntary and professional experience, she has become a specialist in the field of medical transportation. In 1977 Marge enrolled in an EMT (Emergency Medical Technician) program sponsored by the New Jersey Department of Health. Participants in this program were tested by doctors and other health specialists before being certified as members of a Mobile Intensive

Care Unit. In July 1978 Marge became a certified paramedic. Through her voluntary experience and professional training, Marge teaches cardiopulmonary resuscitation (CPR) courses for the American Heart Association and crash management courses for the New Jersey State Police Academy in Sea Girt, New Jersey, as part of the EMT program.

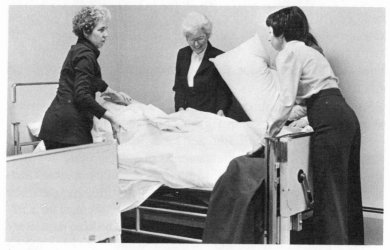

A training session for home health aides.

In 1977 Marge applied for the position of assistant director through the Area Office on Aging and was hired. The project was delayed in starting but slowly acquired four specially equipped vehicles to transport handicapped children and older adults. These vehicles have sliding doors, low-step entrances, and various other features for handicapped patrons. By 1979 the project had acquired eleven vehicles and had become known for its low cost and its efficiency. Funds for the program are provided by the Ocean County Area Office on Aging and other county agencies.

Are there disadvantages in a job involving transportation of older adults? Marge's job can require long hours. Often elderly patrons will call her late at night to ask to be taken to the hospital the next day. The drivers may also call Marge to talk over a problem in the delivery or pickup of older adults. An advantage of the job is the fact that Marge receives many thank-you notes from elderly patients who have been driven to hospitals or to a doctor's office by the friendly and efficient drivers who work for the project.

Marge emphasizes that the field of medical transportation is growing rapidly. Yet it is a new field, and there are few programs concerned with this specialty on the college level. Community colleges and adult education agencies are beginning to offer both credit and noncredit courses in this field. However, one must usually obtain training through voluntary experience. The civil service title of Marge's position is coordinator of nonemergency transportation. It requires four years of college and three years of professional experience. For those persons interested in this type of work, it is challenging and rewarding.

Outreach services are another basic part of the Area Office on Aging. Outreach services are related to information and referral programs, which provide a means of matching and linking older adults with appropriate agencies in the community. They also provide services at the older adult's home such as visiting nurses, home health aides, and home-delivered meals.

Wanda Tugman is Director of Senior Outreach Services for Catholic Family and Community Services in Paterson, New Jersey, a program supported in part by funds from the Area Office on Aging. At twenty-six Wanda has a wide and varied background in working with older adults. While a sophomore at Trenton State College she worked at Trenton Psychiatric Hospital as a social work aide. During this time she also gained experience working with the city and county welfare board of Passaic County, New Jersey. Transferring to Kean College, in Union, New Jersey, Wanda graduated in 1975 with a bachelor's degree in social work. In 1976 she became a medical social worker for Hackensack Hospital and also worked for the Paterson Board of Health. In September 1979 Wanda became an outreach worker, and in July 1980 she took her present post.

The nine outreach workers whom Wanda supervises try to locate older persons, assess their needs, and connect them with the appropriate services in the community. Finding some older adults takes energy and persistence. It means door-to-door canvassing, especially in neighborhoods where older and poorer adults live. It means contacting community agencies and persons who work with older adults such as nurses, doctors, pharmacists, and others.

As Wanda points out, people enter the field of gerontology because of personal commitment or by chance. If they enter it by chance they may become very enthusiastic about the field after a while. In Wanda's case, she had a three-generation family and saw her mother quit her job to take care of her grandmother.

What type of personality should you have to be successful in this field? In order to be effective in working with older adults, Wanda says, you must know yourself. "I am most successful when I am comfortable with myself and am able to give completely to the older adult. If you have any fears or hangups they will come out when you are working with older adults." According to Wanda, older adults are very open and frank with you, and you must be the same way with them. In order to help an older man, Wanda says, she had to work through her own fear of death and dying before she could effectively counsel him about his own fears of dying.

What are the advantages and disadvantages of working with older adults? In obtaining funds for programs for older adults, Wanda believes that the elderly themselves are very helpful. They are retired and have the time necessary to be active in politics, and they are a good support group for laws and programs that benefit older adults. Wanda believes that the passage of the Older Americans Act of 1965 helped focus attention on older adults and their need for programs and services.

But there are disadvantages in working with older adults. Wanda points out that it is not necessarily true that one becomes senile as one ages. However, because of the way many older adults have been treated by society, they tend to view themselves as inferior and lacking in skills. Often they reject the services that Wanda and her outreach workers offer, tending to accept their life as it is.

For someone entering this field, Wanda advises obtaining varied experience in social work. She especially advises obtaining a job before you finish your education. Classroom theory and real-life experience may be quite different. Wanda is presently enrolled in a master's degree program in social work administration at Rutgers University, New Brunswick, N.J., and enjoys working with older adults and dealing with their total needs.

The Area Agency on Aging itself can be a source of jobs for young people. The agency in a large city or county includes many kinds of positions. In New York City, for example, there are five separate bureaus. The Bureau of Direct Services includes information and referral services, Foster Grandparent programs, and community concerns. The Bureau of Community Programs supervises recreation, nutrition, and home care programs in each borough. The Bureau of Research and Policy Analysis includes persons who have a knowledge of grant writing and applying for Federal funds. Programs concerned with employment and crime prevention are in operation in each borough. The Administrative section includes personnel who are accountants, computer programmers, and management information specialists. Persons with specialized job skills can apply for jobs in their field where they can utilize their training for the benefit of older adults.

Randy Goldstein, assistant to the Director of the New York City Office on Aging, obtained her job by hard work, persistence, and the necessary education and training. In 1974 Randy enrolled as a psychology major at the State University of New York in Buffalo. After two years, she decided to enter a more direct service program and transferred to Columbia University in New York City for a program in social work. In 1976 Randy received her bachelor's degree in social work. Upon graduation she applied for a job with the Department of Aging in New York City but was turned down. She decided to enroll in a master's degree program in social work at

Columbia and during her second year in the program applied for an internship with the Department of Aging. From September 1977 to May 1978, for three days a week, Randy aided in developing evaluation methods for programs in home care for older adults. She also performed site visits and evaluated community programs. In May 1978 she applied for a job with the Department of Aging and was again turned down. In the following month, however, an entry-level position as a paraprofessional became available. Randy immediately accepted this position, which involved job assessment and personnel counseling of older adults. In May 1979 an opening in the Department of Aging occurred that required the master's in social work that Randy had previously obtained. Randy applied for and obtained the job of program manager. In this position Randy participated in the renovation of senior centers to enable handicapped people to use the facilities. The job included coordination with state offices, community development offices in the city, and the Department of Housing and Urban Development in Washington, DC. It also required trips to the state capitol in Albany. As a result Randy met Janet Sainer, the director of the New York City Office on Aging, and in January 1980 she was asked to join the director's staff as an assistant. In two years Randy moved from an entry-level job to a position of responsibility in one of the largest Area Offices on Aging in the country.

Her primary job is confidential assistant to the director. She prepares correspondence and drafts replies to correspondence for the director. She is responsible for monitoring and implementing grants awarded by the New York City Office on Aging. She acts as liaison between the New York City Office and the Administration on Aging in Washington. She acts as adviser to the Advisory Council of the New York City Office, preparing agendas for meetings, interpreting city and state mandates for the Council, and following up on recommendations made by the Council. She also acted as the New York City technical coordinator for the White House Conference on Aging held in 1981.

How did Randy's interest in aging arise? Randy always had close contact with her grandparents. When she was growing up she used to visit her grandmother in a nursing home at least three or four times a week. Her grandmother lived to be 93, and the conditions that Randy observed in the nursing home made a strong impression on her. Randy was also the youngest of twenty-one grandchildren and a favorite of both of her grandparents. In high school in New York City, Randy did volunteer work with the Urban Corps and with the Workman's Circle, a nursing home in the Bronx. Later in college, she continued her interest in aging as a volunteer at the Buffalo State Psychiatric hospital and as a case worker at the Jewish Home and Hospital in New York City.

What does Randy advise if you are interested in this field? A good entry-level job in social services is that of a caseworker in a senior center or nursing home. You can obtain a bachelor's degree in social work and qualify yourself to perform this type of work. However, the job market is restricted and you will have to seek out available openings. You might also apply for a position as program monitor or program specialist, in which you monitor or evaluate programs at community agencies that have been awarded grants by your Area Office on Aging. You might also become a program officer in the agency. In some cities, such as New York, salaries will be based on union agreements.

There are other positions that you can qualify for through education or experience. Many of the professional positions require a master's degree in social work with three years' experience in the aging field. Some require specialized training in public administration, nutrition, senior center administration, or research in aging.

When asked whether it is possible to move from one job in aging to another, Randy pointed out that it is not always possible because of the specialized nature of the field. However, a social service background is important. It is difficult to move up or obtain promotions without training in social service. There is need for public administration graduates and community planners. At the present time, the delivery of health services to older adults in the community is receiving priority. Therefore job openings in health planning and health administration will continue to increase.

The career positions that have been described all demonstrate that young women displaying initiative can rise to positions of leadership in the aging field. The methods by which these workers obtained their jobs varied. Some took summer jobs, some gained experience through college supervised internships, and some by working for a number of social service agencies. Others simply saw an announcement in the newspaper and through having the necessary qualifications obtained the job. In a number of instances, these workers started in entry-level positions and were paid relatively low salaries, but they gained the experience and knowledge that they needed.

For the positions mentioned in this chapter, how much money is earned? A lawyer working in a public agency earns between $14,000 and $20,000 per year. A transportation coordinator in a New Jersey civil service position earns approximately $11,500 to $16,000. An outreach director who works for a private nonprofit agency earns between $10,000 and $14,000. In a larger agency, a director of outreach programs would receive a higher salary. Program monitors in New York City earn between $15,000 and $20,000. The holder of this type of position might be a food service or nutrition specialist with a bachelor's degree in nutrition or food service management and two years of experience. A person with the required experience in the field of aging and a master's degree in social work could earn $18,000 to start in large cities and urban areas. For specialized fields such as accounting, computer programming, or systems analysis, a trainee with a BA and experience in the field could start at a relatively high salary, depending on local and regional supply and demand.

*Chapter* **IV**

---

# Senior Centers

Today the senior center is a gathering place for older adults in many cities and towns in the United States. There are over *10,000* such centers in cities and towns throughout the United States, providing information and referral services and activities that seniors need. The senior center helps older adults to remain active and channels their skills and abilities into productive activities. The senior center not only serves the healthy older adult but also provides supportive services for older people as they become frail or ill. It usually works in cooperation with other community agencies and organizations to provide a wide range of services for older adults.

Most senior centers have a program services unit, a social services unit, and a health services unit. Some provide special services such as adult day-care services, congregate nutrition programs, or in-home care. But in most centers, social, recreational, and educational activities are the heart of the daily operation. Many centers program activities such as music, crafts, square dancing, adult education classes, choral groups, sewing, woodworking, physical fitness, dramatics, ballroom dancing, and painting. They invite speakers from the community, provide film series, and plan and conduct day trips to places of interest.

What does the social services section of a senior center do? Usually these services are carried out by a professional social worker whose staff provides personal and family counseling, crisis intervention, services to handicapped seniors, outreach, Social Security counseling, assistance in filing tax forms, and information and referral services.

The health services unit is designed to discover and prevent health risks and illnesses in older adults. Often a health education program or health screening service helps seniors discover health risks and personal illness. Health screening means checking blood pressure, providing for vision or hearing checks, and emphasizing the importance of foot care.

An employment counselor works with an older adult.

While many senior centers operate only five days a week, some multipurpose centers in large cities may operate seven days a week. The Waxter Senior Center in Baltimore, Maryland, is an example of a seven-day center. Waxter has a large staff of professionals who attempt to provide programs for the handicapped as well as the healthy. At Waxter seventy blind seniors and forty deaf seniors participate in its varied programs.

Since the number of frail older adults who participate in activities at senior centers is increasing, Waxter has started a physiotherapy program and an occupational therapy program. Many senior centers find a growing need for a director of health services. Jack Gleason, Director of Health Services at Waxter, has spent most of his career in that field. Before joining Waxter in 1974, he was administrator of a pediatrics unit at the University of Maryland Hospital in Baltimore, and he previously worked for the National Tuberculosis Association in Washington, DC.

As director of health services, what are Jack's responsibilities? Jack is in contact with all community agencies that are willing to provide health services for seniors at the center. The most important part of the program is a comprehensive health screening service. Each year about 1,500 seniors are given a complete physical examination. After a physician reviews the records, referrals are made to outside health agencies in the Baltimore area. Jack coordinates the service, refers seniors to the agencies, and makes sure they have made and kept their appointments.

Jack also coordinates with universities and colleges in the area to bring interns in the health services field to provide health services for seniors and at the same time experience for students. For example, the University of Maryland Dental School and its Dental Hygiene School provide services for Waxter participants. Graduate psychology students offer group sessions in mental health for recently widowed participants. Waxter also has a contract with the Maryland Podiatry Association for two student interns to come to Waxter and provide foot care for older adults. Other health services that are provided include physical therapay, vision, hearing, and speech services. Coordination of health services for older adults is becoming an important responsibility of senior centers, and the number of health care administrators should increase as the centers attempt to provide services for the handicapped or frail.

There are many varied kinds of jobs and positions with senior centers, depending on the size of the center. A small neighborhood center may have only a director, a secretary, a van driver, and additional temporary help from community employment programs or volunteers from the community. A center as large as Waxter may have a director, an assistant director, an educational director, a staff of social workers, an employment director, a legal services director, and many other employees.

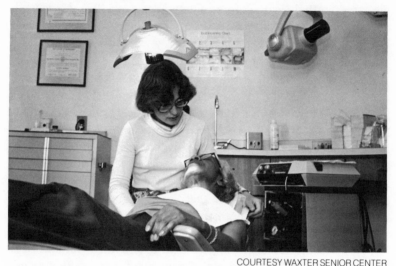

COURTESY WAXTER SENIOR CENTER

A participant receives a dental checkup at a senior center.

Social workers are extremely important to the senior center. As a social worker you will be developing a service plan, identifying the needs of participants at the center, and making referrals or contacts with other health care personnel. Often the older adult may need the services of an occupational therapist or a psychiatrist. Usually the social worker must have a broad knowledge of community agencies that provide services for older adults. At times the social worker is the person who provides individual contact with the participant and accompanies him or her to a community agency to obtain needed services.

Most centers have a food and nutrition program that provides a daily hot lunch for participants. Some also have a food shopping service in which members are driven to a supermarket and then back home with their purchases. Administration of such a program requires a degree in nutrition or dietetics and knowledge of food purchasing, cooking, and weight control.

All senior centers have someone who is in charge of program activities. In a small center, it may be the director who fills this post. In large centers, someone will be designated as program director, activities director, or education director. Kathy Murphy is Assistant Director of the Bergen County Multipurpose Center in Midland Park, New Jersey. Her responsibilities include planning programs, ordering supplies, and scheduling activities. She also is involved in providing arts and crafts programs and has started an exercise class. Kathy enjoys planning programs for seniors. She says, "Each one must find their own strength and use it at the center. In order to work with seniors, you must be flexible, have an outgoing personality, and see that things move smoothly. Sometimes seniors will discuss their personal problems with you. When this occurs, you will have to identify the most important problem that seems to be bothering them. You may be able to provide information or refer them to a local community agency for help." Kathy offers this advice: "Don't jump to conclusions and don't allow their problems to overwhelm you. Many of the participants of the center have been living for seventy or eighty years without your help. Most seniors are not helpless and can manage their own affairs."

COURTESY WAXTER SENIOR CENTER

An art therapist works with participants at a senior center.

Where did Kathy obtain her experience in working with older adults? Kathy started out in her senior year in high school as a part-time dietary aide or weekend cook in a nursing home. When the recreation director was absent or ill, Kathy also substituted for her. During her junior year at Saint Thomas Aquinas College in Sparkill, New York, Kathy attended a career workshop in gerontology. As a result, she decided to enter the field of gerontology and graduated in 1975 with a BS in psychology and a minor in gerontology. While attending college, she continued to work part time in a nursing home. Upon graduation she was employed by the visiting homemakers service in Bergen County. Her duties consisted of identifying homebound elderly people, visiting them, and helping them with personal chores and shopping. Then she obtained a position with the Bergen County Office on Aging as an information and referral assistant. Her job consisted of providing information to older adults about programs and services in the area. Shortly thereafter she obtained her present position.

Her nursing home experience has given her objectivity in working with older adults. As Kathy points out, success is more quickly obvious when you are working with young people, but you will see learning and growth in participants at a senior center. On the other hand, a disadvantage of working with older adults is that those who become your best friends may become ill or die. Nevertheless, Kathy enjoys the challenges of working at the center and the variety of experiences that each day brings.

Not all jobs at a senior center involve working directly with programs for participants. A successful senior center program usually results from good administrative and support personnel. Leigh A. Schade, Business Manager of the Lockport Senior Center in Lockport, New York, started out as a secretary at the center and in five years rose to her present position.

As Leigh points out, one of the most difficult parts of her job is to identify and apply to various state and Federal agencies that provide funds for senior centers. In addition to being a budget director, a business manager must know the total program and activities of the center. She must be able to describe what kinds of activities are taking place at the center in budgetary terms.

One of Leigh's main tasks is educating the staff on the importance of program cost. At in-service training sessions, Leigh discusses the program of the center in budgetary terms. The cost of each service must be calculated. Very often with the high cost of gasoline, the staff of a center must keep transportation costs to a minimum.

Not all older adults are retired. Here, an over-65 senior receives job counseling.

Each member of the center is part of a team. For instance, Leigh supervises a staff that includes a bookkeeper, a secretary, and a part-time accountant who is a senior citizen. Their responsibility is to monitor and keep track of the budget at the center, but they often take on additional responsibilities. As participants become familiar with staff members and see them every day, they often discuss personal problems. Sometimes the staff must be able to refer participants to the proper service or facility in the center or in the community. Their ability to listen to a center participant may be more important than their skill as a bookkeeper or secretary. As Leigh points out, you must care about helping people and gain personal satisfaction from working with older adults to be an effective employee at the center.

Leigh had ten years of experience in private industry and in hospitals prior to joining the Lockport Senior Center, but she does not expect to return to private industry. She says, "Once you start in a senior center, you're hooked on working in this type of facility." Leigh is currently enrolled in a program leading to a bachelor's degree in business administration from Empire State University, the external degree college that is part of the State University of New York.

If you are interested in positions in a senior center that require accounting or budgetary skills, a degree in business administration would be helpful. At the same time you should obtain some knowledge of human relations through courses in sociology or psychology.

Many senior centers have a staff member who is in charge of coordinating volunteers. Gina Bowditch is the director of volunteers at the Mon-Yough Senior Center in McKeesport, Pennsylvania. Sometimes volunteers lack information concerning their position or the goals of the agency in which they are volunteers. Gina's job is to define roles, clarify positions, train volunteers, and insure that they have a clear picture of the agency or department in which they volunteer. She also writes job descriptions so that each volunteer will know what his or her task is. Gina also coordinates the activities of volunteers, supervises the senior companion program, and helps write a newsletter that is distributed to the center participants.

At twenty-five, Gina has been trained in the field of gerontology. In 1977 she graduated from Penn State University with a bachelor's degree in human development and a gerontology minor. Her courses in psychology and sociology included an internship in a nursing home. She also had previous volunteer experience with older adults. She was an ACTION volunteer for three years, a nurse's aide for six months, and worked in a nursing home as a volunteer. Her mother had been coordinator of a meals on wheels program for older adults, in which Gina participated.

For those persons considering a career in the field of aging, Gina suggests that they gain volunteer experience. She also suggests that if you decide to major in gerontology in college, you take courses that will include skills you will be able to utilize in working with older adults, such as courses in psychology and sociology. There will be repetition in the coursework at times, but the emphasis on human development will help you. She also suggests that courses in statistics will be helpful in a job where record-keeping or records management is one of your tasks.

Not all jobs at a senior center require college training or a graduate degree. Perhaps you are a college student or a housewife with limited skills or limited time to work. You can find out if you like working with older adults by taking a job as a driver for a senior center. Of course you must have a valid license for the area in which you live, and you must be ready to drive a large van or a car depending upon the number of older adults you will be transporting. Peggy Pettis has been a driver at the Mon-Yough Senior Center for four years. Peggy says that the main qualification for a driver is "patience and more patience." You will also need to be familiar with the various facilities that are used by older adults. You will often have to take participants to nutrition sites, to medical appointments, and to government offices such as Social Security or agencies that provide energy assistance.

There are advantages and disadvantages to being a driver at a senior center. You will like socializing with your passengers and getting to know them and discussing the problems of their families and friends. On the other hand, as Peggy points out, you will feel sorry when you learn that one of the participants you carried has become ill or died. You will also be out in all kinds of weather, and sometimes the driving conditions will be difficult.

Sometimes you can gain experience in a senior center through a student internship. The senior center must be willing to assign someone on their staff to supervise and coordinate your work schedule. But through taking such an assignment you can learn what it is like to work in a senior center. Ron Robertson received his bachelor's degree in social work from Stockton State College in Stockton, New Jersey, in June 1980. As part of his academic program, he was expected to devote two days a week to a student internship position. Ron served as an outreach worker in the Saint Francis Senior Center in Brant Beach, New Jersey, a resort area on Long Beach Island, near Atlantic City. Year-round residents include older adults who are in need of programs and services. Ron's job as a student intern was to identify seniors in the community, find out their problems, and determine whether they were eligible for various services. These services included food stamps, meals on wheels, and others. In his year as an outreach worker, he spent most of his time in the community rather than at the center. However, he learned about the role of a senior center in the community, and he obtained academic credit for his learning experience. Most important, he was able to help older adults and sometimes act as an advocate for them to obtain the services that they required.

## SENIOR CENTER DIRECTORS

The responsibilities of the director of a senior center depend on the type of facility. It may be a neighborhood center, a multipurpose center in a suburban area, or an inner-city center where the director supervises a large staff.

If you decided that you would like to become director of a senior center, what type of training or experience would you need? Of the three centers mentioned in this chapter, each director has undergraduate or graduate training in social service as well as years of professional experience in the field of aging.

Mary Jane Lyman, Director of the Waxter Senior Center in Baltimore, Maryland, supervises one of the largest senior center programs in the country. The current membership at Waxter is approximately 9,000, and a staff of fifty full-time employees and thirty part-time employees work with older adults who come to the center daily.

Mary Jane started as a volunteer with the Lutheran Social Service Agency in Baltimore. Her volunteer experience included setting up three meals on wheels programs for older adults. She also worked for the Health and Welfare Council of Baltimore as a research assistant. Then she continued to work for the Lutheran Social Services Agency, performing congregation and community development work in public housing for seniors. Later she worked as community coordinator for Title III programs for the Maryland State Commission on Aging. Shortly thereafter, Leon Wolf, Director of the Waxter Senior Center, asked Mary Jane to become Assistant Director. Mary Jane has been at Waxter since 1974 and became Director in 1979. She has over ten years' experience in the field of aging.

Wilma Casella is Director of the Northwest Bergen Multipurpose Senior Center in Bergen County, located in Midland Park, New Jersey. This center provides programs and services to older adults in more than ten communities. Wilma's previous experience includes the job of planner with the Bergen County Office on Aging. Her graduate training in social service includes a master's degree in social work from Fordham University in New York City. Her public affairs activities include service on the Board of Education in Midland Park, and as senior center representative from New Jersey for the National Council on Aging. In 1979 Wilma became founding director of the center in Midland Park.

Linda Van Buskirk is Director of the Senior Center in Lockport, New York, near Buffalo. Linda graduated from Case Western University in Cleveland, Ohio, with a master's degree in social work and in 1974 became a consultant at the Center to help develop programs for older adults. In 1975 she became Director of Counseling and in 1980 she became Director of the center. She replaced Betty Dale, founding director of the center, who retired after twenty-eight years in the field of aging. Lockport is a large urban center that provides programs for all types of older adults. Its facilities include a guidance center, a day-care program for older adults, and many varied programs.

All of these directors make use of their community organization skills, their advocacy ability, and their knowledge of programs and services for older adults. Each senior center program is unique to the area that it serves and the older adults that participate. Each center is a reflection of its community and the personality of its director. In addition, these directors deal with local, county, state and Federal officials in obtaining funds for staff personnel, programs, and facilities. They also have used or are using their knowledge and background to serve on national committees concerned with developing policy in the field of aging.

Salaries for senior center personnel and directors vary widely depending on location and type of agency. In general, salaries are higher on the East and West coasts. In 1975 the National Council on Aging completed a survey of salaries for senior center directors and discovered that the median salary was approximately $10,000. Since then the number of centers has grown tremendously and the responsibilities of directors have expanded. Nevertheless, a small neighborhood senior center might start a director at a salary of $10,000 to $12,000. Salaries for directors of multipurpose centers would range from $14,000 to $18,000. Salaries for senior center directors in large urban areas or cities would range between $18,000 and $28,000.

*Chapter* **V**

---

# Community Programs for Older Adults

One of the main tasks of agencies that work with older adults is to provide services and programs to enable frail, handicapped, or ill seniors to remain on their own in the community. Any service that will help the older adult to continue to be independent is much in demand. A low-cost service that is available in most communities is the homemaker or home health aide service. This service provides in-home services to adults who have recently been discharged from the hospital after illness, accident, or surgery and need help in coping or caring for themselves.

Visiting homemakers or home health aides usually complete a short intensive training program that is certified by the county or state in which they work. In addition, they receive continuous in-service training from the agency in which they work. They are usually supervised by registered nurses and social workers. Their duties include home care of the patient such as helping with bathing, getting in and out of bed, and doing prescribed exercises. In many cases the aide helps the patient to practice regaining speech, relearn household skills, or engage in special activities that have been prescribed. They usually help with eating, including planning and preparation of meals or special diets. They may also accompany the patient to the doctor's office or to a medical facility.

The Visiting Homemaker Service of Ocean County, in Toms River, New Jersey, was started in 1966 as a voluntary nonprofit agency to serve the health and social service needs of Ocean County residents. Its purposes include: allowing aging or disabled persons to remain at home, eliminating the high cost of institutional care, relieving family members of total patient care, and keeping the family intact and enabling family members to continue working.

Mary Feldman, R.N., founded the agency to care for the large number of older adults who live in retirement communities and trailer parks throughout the county. The agency has expanded to keep up with the growing population. It now has over 650 home health aides and a staff of over forty persons who coordinate and supervise the work of aides.

Ann Verb is one of two Area Service Supervisors at this agency. Her task is to supervise the field supervisors and service coordinators who work with the home health aides. She reviews and approves case plans for each patient and reviews field activities through reports, case conferences, and home visits. She plans and holds conferences with visiting homemaker team members. She also interviews and recommends applicants to fill service staff positions.

What qualities do you need to perform the duties of an area service supervisor? Ann feels that you have to be industrious and have a high energy level. You must be honest in dealing with patients and the aides who work with patients in all sorts of family situations, and you must have good organizational ability.

For this position you must be a registered nurse and be able to deal with medical problems that occur in the field. Through staff training and individual counseling, Ann encourages staff members to be warm and friendly in dealing with patients and with aides on the job. Ann states, "Our job is to help people die at home, people with nobody and with no family." Sometimes Ann has the job of firing aides or other staff personnel who have not functioned up to the standards of the agency. It is difficult to do this without damaging the person's self-confidence. Yet Ann must be honest in carrying out this part of her job and deal with the person in terms of his or her own strengths and weaknesses.

## BACKGROUND AND TRAINING

Ann started in her job five years ago and has received much on-the-job training. She believes that her high school experience and college training have helped qualify her for her job. She started working in high school as a nurse's aide in a nursing home. She also worked during the summers as a junior and senior camp counselor with brain-damaged children.

After graduating from high school, Ann briefly attended McGill University in Montreal, Canada, and Case Western University in Cleveland, Ohio. Like many other students, she was unsure of her vocational goal. While a liberal arts student, she applied to Massachusetts General Hospital in Boston for the nursing program. She was accepted and from 1972 to 1975 she attended nursing school and worked at Massachusetts Rehabilitation Hospital in Boston. Upon graduation, she returned to New Jersey and worked briefly at Deborah Hospital in Browns Mills and at Paul Kimball Hospital in Lakewood. She was hired by the Visiting Homemakers Service in 1976. At present she is a student at Thomas Edison College in Trenton, working toward a BS degree in nursing.

What are the disadvantages of Ann's job? She is continually dealing with people in crisis: patients and family members who become emotional or people who become irritable and forgetful. Sometimes aides and patients become too dependent on one another. At times it is easier for the home health aide to do personal tasks rather than training the patient to do them. Patients may begin to call the aide about personal matters rather than home health responsibilities. It is part of Ann's job to ensure that aides are rotated to other patients after six months.

Ann respects her boss, Mary Feldman, and enjoys working for the agency. She says, "I like working here. You function best in an atmosphere of caring."

## GERIATRIC COUNSELING CENTER

A geriatric counseling center usually is associated with a hospital or a senior citizen complex. The Lockport Geriatric Counseling

Center is a unit of the Lockport Senior Center. Its full-time staff includes a director of counseling who is a graduate social worker. Other staff members include social workers, nurses, home help aides, and an occupational therapist. Part-time professional help includes psychologists and a psychiatrist who devote part of their practice to counseling and treating older adults.

Older adults are referred for this service by other social service agencies in the community, by ministers, by hospitals, and by family members. The social worker is one of the most important staff members in the counseling center. Jean Perry is a social worker at the center. Her main task is to identify the needs of older adults and provide help in dealing with agencies or social services in the community. Jean must have a thorough knowledge of those agencies that provide services for the older adult such as Medicaid, Social Security, the food stamp program, and the local housing authority.

Sometimes the older adult just needs someone to listen to his or her problems. If the senior citizen is homebound, Jean will see that social service personnel such as a public health nurse or a home help aide visit and provide in-home services. For the healthy older adults, Jean acts as a contact with the center. As she says, "It's very important to steer them into activities at the center in which they can be successful."

Jean has a BS degree in biology. She has worked as a social worker designee in a nursing home and has previous experience as an outreach worker at the center.

Other staff personnel who are important in helping the older adult remain in the community include the home help aide and the occupational therapist. Usually an occupational therapist is based in a hospital or nursing home and works with patients in those settings. Eileen Hertz, O.T., is the occupational therapist at the Lockport Center. In order to work as an occupational therapist with older adults, Eileen believes that you need a background in arts and crafts, an understanding of human behavior, a good knowledge of your profession, and the ability to put yourself in the place of the

Maimonides, Donna has participated in seminars, in-service training, analytic training, and psychodrama training, all of which have enabled her to improve her skills in group counseling. She also conducts in-service training sessions for nurses at the hospital. One of her main tasks is educating nursing staff and other personnel in mental health problems.

As a psychiatric nurse or social worker, one of the disadvantages of working with older adults is that you may not be able to make major changes in their life-style. You can help them recognize and deal with their problems, together setting goals and objectives for them; however, it may be difficult for them to achieve the goals, and sometimes the goals will have to be modified.

Another disadvantage of working with older adults is that a patient with whom you have worked very closely may become ill and die. This would be less likely to happen if you had been working with young people.

In working with older adults, the community mental health worker is dealing with losses. If a husband becomes ill or suffers from a physical or mental handicap, the worker must know what services may help so that the wife can continue to cope with the situation. Wives may need counseling because the husband experiences memory loss and needs strong support services from the community.

Abraham Marin is a mental health worker at Maimonides who came to Brooklyn from Puerto Rico sixteen years ago. During that time he has been a housekeeping aide, a superviser of housekeeping, a messenger, a printer, and a mental health worker. Maimonides sent him for six months' training as a mental health worker. In addition, Abraham has attended classes at New York Community College and Staten Island Community College. Abraham enjoys being part of the mental health team. He says he learned from many health professionals since coming to the hospital. However, there are disadvantages in being a mental health worker. Abraham points out, "The work can be dangerous. You are working with disturbed adults. They may be schizophrenics or

older adult.

The main function of an occupational therapist is to help older adults improve in activities for daily living. This includes hand skills for dressing, cooking, cleaning, and leisure activities. Eileen also helps seniors set individual goals and develops a meaningful program for each person she works with. For example, if an older adult is visually handicapped, he or she must be helped to improve shopping skills or money changing in order to take care of finances. In one instance, Eileen made a stencil that the older adult could use to put the entries in the right places on bank checks. Other aids include special magnifiers to help older adults continue to sew or operate other home appliances.

Eileen likes her job at the center. It is different from her hospital experience. In a hospital, when patients get well they return home, and you do not always see the results of your work. In a geriatric center, you work more closely with older adults in a community setting and see the results of your work.

Another direct service employee who can be attached to a geriatric counseling center or senior center is a home help aide. Mary Seaman is a home help aide at the Lockport center. At twenty-eight, she has over four years' experience in direct service work with older adults. In this job she works with a social worker and takes older adults shopping or performs community chores for and with them. She finds the work interesting and stimulating.

Mary was well trained for her position. She earned a certificate as specialist in gerontology from the University of Buffalo. This included 104 hours of instruction for people who work with older adults. Mary has also taken courses in braille and mobility training to work with blind older adults. As part of her training Mary was blindfolded for an entire day to help her understand what it is like to be visually impaired.

How did Mary become interested in this field? She had worked at various jobs in sales and in retail stores after graduating from high school. She applied for a position as a home health aide and was hired. Her grandmother, who was legally blind, had died at the age of ninety. Perhaps that is why she decided to enter the field of aging.

## COMMUNITY MENTAL HEALTH CENTER

For a long time mental health services for older adults were limited. Mental health practitioners concentrated on younger adults, who they believed could benefit more from psychological therapy. However, in recent years community mental health centers have developed in connection with hospitals as part of their out-patient services. These centers have expanded their services to include counseling of older adults.

The purpose of community mental health centers is twofold. First, it is to identify community members who are developing or exhibiting symptoms of mental illness and treat these persons in the community, thereby reducing the cost of mental health care for the average patient. Second, the community mental health center acts as a link or organization in the community to help former mental patients adjust to community living. In recent years, the Federal government has encouraged states to discharge mental patients from state institutions and return them to the community. The community mental health center has therefore become very important as an agency that provides support, helps the former patient to develop self-confidence, provides information about community resources such as housing, health services, public benefits, jobs, and social groups, and helps in the readjustment to community life.

Donna Sultan is a staff member of the community mental health center at Maimonides Hospital in Brooklyn, New York. Donna is a psychiatric nurse who is trained in providing mental health services for all ages. As a mental health worker, Donna must help the older adult deal with losses of all kinds, including physical, social, and economic losses. She must know what services to obtain for the older adult.

As a mental health worker, Donna counsels and encourages older

adults to be more aggressive in dealing with everyday pr This often means helping them to deal effectively wit' members. It also means helping the passive senior to beco in meeting people and making friends, introducing him programs and services in the community such as a senior nutrition program.

It is true that a social worker on a mental health te form these tasks, but the community nurse is importa ing the health problems of the older adult. The nurse contact the doctor who is treating the older adul medicines or drugs that the older adult is taking. The advise on blood pressure problems, on diuretics, an that may occur from drugs prescribed for the olde tion, a nurse trained in psychiatric counseling can adults to participate in group counseling at the mer Sometimes older adults with no previous history become extremely depressed after retirement an to restore mental health, particularly those wh their lives and have developed no leisure intere

Sometimes the psychiatric nurse or social v training in reality orientation for family m adults are experiencing a severe memory los within the family, the older adult can be helpe tant facts in the home situation.

How do you become a psychiatric nu training, on-the-job training, and academ background includes five years' experienc After graduating from Columbia Univer Donna worked at a psychiatric day hos for two years. Returning to Brooklyn, sl in-patient nurse at Maimonides, where years. During the last three years sh geriatric unit of the hospital. Donna educational psychology from the C'

alcoholics. The goals you set for older adults may not be reached. You must adjust to modified goals and not be disappointed.''

## ADULT DAY-CARE CENTERS

The development of day-care centers for older adults in the United States has been rapid. From only fifteen programs in 1974, by 1980 there were over 600 programs in existence. The purpose of the programs is to provide services with a community setting for isolated or handicapped older adults. An adult day-care center can be used to remove from nursing homes or mental institutions older adults who need only limited care. It can also delay the placing of an older adult in a nursing home or other institutional facility. However, its primary purpose is to help older adults with handicaps to remain in the community, socialize with neighbors and friends, and live independently.

A day-care program for older adults helps to reduce isolation, stimulate interest in leisure activities, and provide opportunities for socializing. It also provides instruction in health care and information and assistance regarding other community agencies. When possible, the staff of a program provide advice and counseling for a family member or someone caring for the participant.

There are two types of day-care centers. A social day-care program provides limited services, primarily social and recreational activities. A medical day-care program provides participants with nursing services, social work services, and health services including physical therapy, occupational therapy, and speech therapy as needed. In most cases such a program must be state-approved for Medicaid. Meals and transportation are usually provided in both types of centers .

Participants in an adult day-care program usually come from the community or have recently been discharged from hospital with some type of disability such as stroke, heart or circulatory disease, diabetes, arthritis, or vision problems. Emphasis is placed on a person's "wellness." Therefore a typical progam concentrates on preventive health planning or helping older adults regain their health.

One may wonder why an older adult needs to come to a day-care center, why he or she can't remain at home and be cared for. It may be that the older adult has no spouse living, no children nearby, no relatives or friends to help. Perhaps he or she lives in an inner city and in poor conditions.

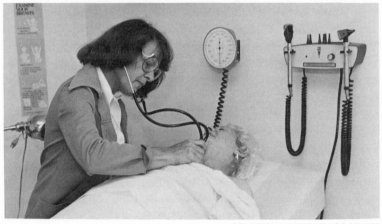

COURTESY WAXTER SENIOR CENTER

Older adults can receive health checkups in senior centers.

Elaine Hinnion, MSW, is director of an adult day-care center in Paterson, New Jersey. The program is administered by the Catholic Family and Community Services Organization in Paterson, whose Director of Aging is Joanne Tuohy. The program serves twenty-five older adults, most of whom live in public housing. The center is a "freestanding center," meaning that it obtains services for its participants from the community and is not part of a hospital or nursing home complex.

What are the main jobs found at a day-care center? Each center has a director, sometimes an assistant director, a social worker, a nurse usually with public health experience, and an activities director who has had therapeutic recreation training.

A competent activities coordinator is important for the day-to-day operation of the center. In Paterson, Dot Mastrian is the instructor in arts and crafts. She chooses activities that will help each participant become independent or self-confident. Very often she must plan activities for participants who have had a stroke and do not feel capable of any activity. Through activities that are easily accomplished, the participant regains confidence and moves on to harder tasks. Participants are often urged to create something that they can be proud of, such as a painting or sculpture, and take home or give to a friend or relative.

Dot Mastrian urges young people to consider employment in day-care centers and senior centers as teachers of older adults. With appropriate training and education, they can motivate many older adults to participate more fully. In coming years there will be many openings and opportunities for advancement for staff personnel.

Most centers have a nurse with public health training. Winnie Kelley is the RN at the Paterson Day Care Center. Her main duties involve counseling participants and encouraging them in self-care of their own health problems. She believes that physical exercise is important for participants. She leads them each day in simple range of motion exercises that help to extend and flex their body joints. Other exercises help improve their circulation and keep them mobile. If a participant cannot care for himself, he is placed in a nursing home. According to Winnie, a participant can prevent this or delay it by taking part in the therapeutic activities at the center.

*DIRECTOR*

What sort of background should a director of an adult day-care center have? Basic and sometimes as important as a good formal education is a sensitivity to people. An honest caring for older adults is perhaps the most important characteristic necessary for all staff personnel at a day-care center. Elaine Hinnion, Director of the Paterson center, believes that you must have a staff that is patient, caring, and committed. The staff is the key to improving services to each participant.

Elaine says, "The important thing is to get the older adult to risk it." Find out what programs are appropriate for each participant. What is the short-range goal for each? The long-range goal? Elaine first tries to resocialize the participants and then encourages them to start doing things they used to do. This may mean baking, crocheting, teaching, or going to church again. The important thing is to get each participant to regain confidence in him or herself and risk it.

Elaine believes that the philosophy of an adult day-care center is to make each participant independent. For that reason as many services as needed are provided for each participant—companion and escort, outreach, meals on wheels—but then services are reduced to allow the participant to live and act independently.

Elaine's extensive background in working with community organizations helps her carry out responsibilities as director. She has worked in a child welfare agency, an adoption agency, and for six years in a mental health clinic. This experience helps her identify resources in Paterson that can be utilized by the center for the needs of each participant. This includes agencies for the blind, for arthritis, diabetes, and cancer. It includes homemaker services, housing authority, department of health, and community agencies willing to provide programs or services for the participants of the day center.

## *ASSISTANT DIRECTOR*

As indicated, some day-care centers have an assistant director. Drew Goeb is Assistant Director of the Day Care Center at Waxter Senior Center in Baltimore, Maryland. Drew helps plan group and individual activities for participants at the center. A group craft project may be started that enables each participant to contribute to the best of his ability, encouraging and promoting resocialization. The participants may also take part in individual education classes at Waxter.

Drew did not plan to be involved in the aging field when he graduated from high school. He first worked for the Bethlehem Steel Company in production work. After two years he decided to return to school, and in 1976 he graduated from Towson State College in Towson, Maryland, with a BA in psychology. He started in project transition at Waxter, which involved making home assessments of frail older adults and determining what services they needed. Later he became project coordinator and after eighteen months moved to his present position as Assistant Director.

Drew is confident of his future in working with older people. Although the staff of adult day-care centers are relatively low-paid, Drew says this is because the field is new and only slowly developing. As Drew points out, over 20 percent of the population of the United States will be over sixty-five in 2025, and therefore the number of jobs in the field of aging will continue to expand.

## SALARIES

Home health aides are relatively low-paid part-time personnel. Some agencies pay them on an hourly basis at $3.50 to $4.00 per hour. Annually this would mean between $5,000 and 6,000, with the top salaries in the large cities. Home help aides earn about the same amount. Social workers in senior centers earn between $13,000 and $18,000. Occupational therapists on a national level earn between $12,000 and $14,000. A registered nurse with psychiatric experience in a large urban hospital earns between $18,000 and $24,000. Nonprofit agencies pay a supervisor of home health aides about $15,000 to $16,000. Directors of day-care centers earn between $16,000 and $22,000. An assistant director earns somewhat less—$12,000 to $14,000.

Chapter **VI**

# Institutionalized Older Adults

There are many jobs associated with caring for older adults in institutions or agencies throughout the country. The most generally known facility for institutional care for persons who are not able to care for themselves or remain in the community in independent living arrangements is the nursing home, convalescent center, or long-term care facility.

There are different kinds of nursing homes or long-term care facilities. Some are operated like any other business, for a profit. Others are nonprofit establishments often sponsored by a church denomination or charitable organization. Some convalescent homes are former county homes that have been converted to long-term care facilities. Usually the staff of these facilities are county civil service employees and come under state civil service rules and regulations.

In a long-term care facility there is a need for physical therapists, occupational therapists, speech therapists, dietary consultants, registered nurses, licensed practical nurses, accountants, and secretaries and bookkeepers in the main office. Large facilities have a director of maintenance and a director of housekeeping. Although certain professional people may not spend all of their working hours in a long-term care facility, they may treat a substantial number of older adults as part of their regular practice. This would include professionals such as doctors, dentists, audiologists, and podiatrists.

If you do not have the necessary education or training to be a professional, it is still possible to obtain a position in a long-term care facility. Perhaps you decide you want to work in a long-term care facility while attending high school or college. What part-time jobs can you obtain? Lower-level jobs will not be easy, nor will the pay be high. Nevertheless you can gain experience as a nurse's aide, a housekeeping aide, or a dietary aide.

You will find that every employee is important in a nursing home, from the manager or administrator to the housekeeper or custodian. All of these employees come into daily contact with the patients or residents, and all must enjoy helping people.

One of the advantages of being employed in a nursing home is that you will be able to work on weekends. You can work every Saturday or Sunday and still go to school during the week. You can also work during the summer and gain experience and training. Most administrators will be willing to work out a flexible work schedule so that you can attend school and continue to work. If there are no nursing homes near you, you might try to find a job in a large hospital to gain experience in a health-care facility. Then you should be able to transfer to a long-term care facility.

## *ADMINISTRATOR*

Many skills are needed to become a competent administrator. Because human relations skills are important, some administrators have backgrounds as ministers or social workers. Without sound business training you will not be able to manage your facility. Therefore, accounting and business training are important. Certainly experience in engineering or building management is useful. During your career you will deal with building construction, air conditioning systems, boiler operation, and energy costs. With a background in these areas, you can spot deficiencies and help reduce building operation costs.

As an administrator you will need human relations skills. Compassion, understanding, and patience are needed in abundance. If you are nervous or high-strung, nursing home employment probably isn't for you. As an administrator you will need to know your staff and your patients. You should try to learn the name of each patient. Patient care comes first in a nursing home. If your facility provides good nursing care, all of the other departments will be of the highest quality. In addition, the way you treat each member of your staff is important. It is worthwhile to visit the nursing home at night or plan to work at least one evening a month to get to know those staff members who are employed during evening hours.

As a nursing home administrator you will be called upon to follow Federal and state regulations. You will be expected to be familiar with guidelines concerning Medicare and Medicaid. You will have to read and review manuals concerned with fire safety, nursing service, housekeeping, pharmaceuticals, medical records, and nutrition. You will have to determine the cost of caring for each of your patients under various levels of care. You will also have to determine costs for each of your departments including dietary, nursing, housekeeping, and building maintenance.

Although you may have a strong interest in working in long-term care facilities, you may find that work in a nursing home is not for you. You will not know whether you are equipped to work with older adults until you actually do so. Some employees find out very quickly that working with older adults is not for them. Every day you will be faced with death, with infirmity, and with crisis situations concerning patients and family, and it may depress you.

Your personal involvement will depend upon the size of the facility in which you are employed. With a small facility you will be personally involved. With a large facility, you will be administering a business and delegating responsibility. In this case you must have the ability to choose a good staff, train them, and let them be responsible for their part in running the nursing home.

## *RECREATION THERAPIST*

Perhaps one of the most important positions in the long-term care facility is the director of recreation or patient activities. In this post you will be in charge of recreational therapists, recreational aides, and volunteers. In large facilities, you may use dance therapists, music therapists, and art therapists to contribute to your program.

COURTESY ARNOLD WALTERS NURSING HOME

Meals at day care centers are times for socializing.

Joan Lefkowitz, Director of Recreational Therapy at Kingsbridge Heights Convalescent Center in New York City, indicates that your job will be to encourage teamwork and coordination among members of your staff. Each member of the staff must be familiar with the problems of each patient and share this information with other staff members. You should have a varied program that includes large group activities, small group activities, and individual activities. Some persons will not participate in your program because they have been loners most of their life and enjoy being by themselves.

One of the activities that you will be involved in is reality orientation for the patient. Reality orientation is an attempt to reinforce everyday reality to the patient. Stress is put on such things as the day of the week, the month, what town the patient is in, repeating the patient's name to the group, and encouraging each patient to contribute and discuss daily events and be less concerned with himself.

Recreational activities include many community activities. A recreational therapist is involved in escorting patients out of the facility. He takes them to a picnic, to a park, to the shore or lake in summer, and to a Christmas tree lighting ceremony in winter. Perhaps some of the patients will attend community events or meetings with other older adults in the community.

Within the facility, a recreational therapist will work with the director of food service to have specialized menus for patients on holidays. These might include Saint Patrick's Day and Valentine's Day programs and programs for all major holidays including Thanksgiving, Christmas, and Easter.

As Charlotte Mosher, Director of Recreational Therapy at Summit Nursing Home in Lakewood, New Jersey, says, you have to be a special kind of person to be a recreational therapist. It is not a nine-to-five job. You must forget that the residents are patients and treat them like people. You will need compassion and patience in working with older adults. You will find that you will work many holidays and weekends. Often you will have to treat Christmas or New Year's as a working day. How about it? Would you be willing to give up holidays and weekends to advance in your profession?

Suppose that you would like to become a recreational therapist in a long-term care facility. What sort of education or training should you obtain? What can you do during your high school years to help you get started in the recreation field? Ruth Bannon is a recreational therapist at Edison Estates Convalescent Center in Edison, New Jersey. Ruth graduated with a BA in recreation from Kean College in 1978. Her specialty was urban and outdoor recreation. At an early age Ruth decided that she wanted to work in recreation. She was a camp counselor and a girl scout leader and visited nursing homes as one of her scout projects in high school. At college she planned programs for students as a member of a college residents association, and she participated in the college recreation club. At age twenty-four, Ruth has been employed in nursing homes for over two years. She points out that you must understand older adults and their biological changes. As Ruth says, "People are people no matter what age they are. Older people and young people are very similar in that both want to talk about their childhood. And older people have lived a long life and they are really 'tired'."

## NURSE

The job of a nurse in a long-term care facility is difficult because the older person has fewer resources than a younger person. The physical resources are diminished, the losses are greater, and the cost of illness for an older person is higher. There are usually multiple losses such as vascular, cerebral, arterial, and bone structure problems with patients in long-term care facilities.

A great deal of compassion is required to work with older adults in a nursing home. Some older adults have been residents for many years. As a nurse you will be expected to spend time with patients and get to know their history. They will consider you their family. In some cases your routine in treating patients may not vary from day to day. You will be expected to maintain each patient at optimum functioning. However, the role of a nurse in a long-term care facility can be very rewarding. Each patient will be very appreciative of your care.

There are also advantages in working as a nurse in a long-term care facility. First you will be working as part of a team. You will work with social services, recreational services, and nursing services. In the team approach, a nurse reviews the goals that have been set for each patient. For each patient, short-term and long-term goals are set. A short-term goal might be to assist the patient to walk ten feet within the facility. A long-term goal might be to help the patient return to the community; however, this goal is accomplished in only a small percentage of cases. As a nurse you can advance and become a head nurse or a supervisor of nurses.

What are the disadvantages? Recently graduated nurses may prefer to work in an acute care hospital in an intensive care unit or an emergency room where life and death decisions are made every minute. They may look down on the day-to-day tasks of the nurse in the long-term facility. Other disadvantages are the large number of records and reports that you must keep. You will be under the observation of state and Federal inspectors who will review the written records of your facility. You will be expected to take in-service courses to keep up to date on the latest trends in your profession. You will also be expected to work weekends and holidays.

What are the other nursing positions in a nursing home? You can become a licensed practical nurse. Usually the training for this position is one year of clinical and classroom work and the passage of a state exam for the licensed practical nurse certificate. Rosemary Callahan is a licensed practical nurse at Lakeland Hospital in Blackwood, New Jersey. For five years Rosemary worked as a nurse's aide at night and attended school during the day. According to her, you must be patient and try to care for each patient as an individual. Many of the patients need remotivation because of apathy and alienation. At twenty-five, Rosemary enjoys working in a nursing home. She feels that she is helping people who are really unable to help themselves.

In many jobs you are expected to have the necessary skills when you begin. This is not true of the job of nurse's aide. You will be trained on the job to do the work. Often jobs for young people are dirty or undignified, but this is not true of the job of nurse's aide. It is cleaner and more dignified than some jobs in a factory or office. However, there are disadvantages. The job can be extremely demanding because you will be lifting, bending, and stretching and dealing with all types of patients.

An important part of the health care team in a long-term care facility is the physical therapist. The physical therapist works on the physical aspects of the patient. The doctor writes a prescription for physical medicine, which includes treatment by heat, light, water, exercise, cold, and sound. All of these possible treatments can be utilized by a physical therapist. A physical therapist can also be considered as similar to a coach or trainer. He aids patients in relearning skills that have been lost through physical disability or limitation.

One of the tasks of the physical therapist is to raise the patient's level of functioning. The patient may be in bed or in a wheelchair. The physical therapist's job will be to advance the patient from a bed to a wheelchair, to a walker, to a cane, and finally to unassisted walking. The therapist performs various types of tests on the patient to determine his disability such as range of motion tests, gross tests, and muscle tests. These tests help the physical therapist to identify the strengths and weaknesses of the patient and to devise an individual program for him or her. In rehabilitating the patient, the physical therapist works as part of the health care team with the physician, nurse, social worker, occupational therapist, and speech therapist.

Robin Kline is a physical therapist at Kingsbridge Heights Convalescent Center in New York City. Robin decided to enter the health care field while in high school. As a volunteer she observed the various professions in several hospitals and decided on a career in physical therapy. Following graduation from Brooklyn College with a BA in psychology, she enrolled in a thirteen-month intensive course in physical therapy for college graduates at Columbia University and graduated as a licensed physical therapist.

According to Robin, there are many opportunities for young people in physical therapy. You can work in general hospitals or in nursing homes. You can work in an orthopedic clinic or in private practice. You can work with persons afflicted with cerebral palsy or other handicaps. You can contract with doctors or community agencies that have home-care programs to visit patients at home. You can work with sports teams or with a physiatrist—a doctor who specializes in rehabilitation medicine. Robin tries to improve range of motion and muscle function in the patients she sees each day. In addition, she tries to strengthen muscles and improve circulation. At twenty-six, Robin is an experienced physical therapist employed at Kingsbridge and also performs consulting work at other agencies.

What are the frustrations that you will experience as a physical therapist? Often you will work with a patient and then he will be discharged from the hospital or nursing home. At home, he will not have the facilities to continue to improve, and in many cases, he will have to return to become your patient again. If you work in a general hospital, you will have the latest equipment available for physical therapy, but if you are employed in a nursing home or visit patients in the community, that may not be true.

Institutions provide recreational activities for residents with the help of volunteers.

Suppose you do not have the time or funds to become a licensed physical therapist. You might consider becoming a physical therapist assistant. A physical therapist assistant works under the direction of a physical therapist. The duties and responsibilities are similar to those of a physical therapist; however, the training is less comprehensive and normally the education required is obtained through a two-year physical therapy assistant program at a community college.

## OCCUPATIONAL THERAPIST

An occupational therapist is one of the key members of the health care team in a long-term care facility. While the physical therapist concentrates on aiding the patient to become ambulatory and walk without assistance, the occupational therapist helps the patient improve in daily living skills. Sometimes the occupational therapist treats not only the physical aspects of the patient but also the mental aspects. For example, an occupational therapist may involve the patient in woodworking to strengthen muscles and provide an outlet for anger and hostility. As an occupational therapist for older adults, you will treat many disabilities such as arthritis, stroke, fracture of a limb, and others. In each instance, you will be treating the whole person.

Betty Williams, supervisor of occupational therapy at Lakeland Hospital in Blackwood, New Jersey, points out that the main purpose of occupational therapy is to increase the patient's ability to perform activities for daily living. Through tests and evaluations, the occupational therapist determines if a patient can use his or her arms, fingers, wrists, and elbows and move various joints. Exercises are prescribed to aid the patient in performing everyday activities such as eating, grooming, dressing, standing up, getting in and out of a chair, and going to the toilet. Because of a stroke, a patient may need to learn to write again, and the occupational therapist will help the patient to develop a new signature. The task of the occupational therapist is to help the older adult become independent.

In some cases the occupational therapist works with the older adult after discharge from a hospital or convalescent center. The therapist visits the home and teaches the patient to use various household appliances, turn lights on and off, open and close windows, and perform other routine household tasks. The O.T. also checks the home and recommends installation of facilities such as railings for bathtubs or supports for toilet facilities to help the older adult cope with everyday living.

You might also become an occupational therapist assistant who works under the supervision of a licensed occupational therapist. As an O.T.A. you will be treating the whole person, encouraging the patient to make decisions in his personal life, to act independently, and to regain confidence.

Recreation can take a practical turn in nursing home programs.

Another type of therapist found in a long-term care facility is the art therapist. The art therapist is generally part of the recreational therapy department. The art therapist is trained to evaluate art work. By involving the patient in painting or other art form the therapist encourages the patient to talk about his work. An older adult who is withdrawn or who cannot speak because of a stroke or other handicap can be encouraged to socialize with other patients by showing his work to them. Art therapists must have a solid knowledge of art and psychology because they relate to older adults through art.

Sue Cristantello is an art therapist at Kingsbridge Heights Convalescent Center in New York City. Through making decisions and planning art projects, Sue helps older adults to gain self-confidence. Sue believes the activity of painting helps reduce feelings of loneliness and aids in resocialization among the patients.

Each patient is different and requires a different approach. Sue encourages patients to make choices about what they wish to paint or draw. Often a discussion of a painting will lead a patient to talk about personal problems. Sue uses the life review method in working with older adults, encouraging them to create pictures of the past, present, and future.

How did Sue decide to become an art therapist? In high school her strongest interest was art and she took many art courses. However, in college she wanted to study psychology. At the College of New Rochelle, in New Rochelle, New York, Sue designed her own major, which included courses in art and psychology. She took a number of courses such as developmental psychology and abnormal psychology, which helped her to understand the problems of individuals from childhood to old age. Before going to Kingsbridge, Sue also worked at the Taconic Correctional Institute in New York State. At twenty-six, she is gaining experience in a new and challenging field.

As Sue points out, there are disadvantages in being an art therapist. It is a new position and is relatively unknown to some staff members in long-term care facilities. Others may resent the role of the art therapist and believe that these functions could be carried out by the staff. Sometimes staff members do not understand how the art therapist can be effectively utilized as part of the health care team.

Suppose you wanted to become an art therapist, where could you obtain work in the field? You might work in rehabilitation centers, in psychiatric and mental facilities, in drug-related programs, and in specialized elementary and secondary school programs. Some art therapists teach and perform research at colleges and universities. Sue has taught courses in art therapy at Pace College in New York City.

## FOOD SERVICE SUPERVISOR

Food is one of the first things that patients complain about in any institution. Complaints are also heard in nursing homes and convalescent centers. Patients are quick to complain about bland, unpalatable food. Lawson June, a food service supervisor at Holmdel Convalescent Center in Holmdel, New Jersey, is aware of patients' needs and provides good food to the staff and residents of the facility.

Lawson has had varied experience to become a food service supervisor. He started as a kitchen helper and then spent ten years as a dietary foreman at Monmouth Medical Center, an acute-care hospital in Long Branch, New Jersey. He also spent two years as a cafeteria manager for Johnson and Johnson, a large industrial plant in New Brunswick, New Jersey. Finally he worked in a restaurant and a nursing home before going to Holmdel as a food service supervisor. At Holmdel he supervises a staff of twenty four, including cooks, relief cooks, senior dietary aides, and dietary aides.

To be an effective food service supervisor, Lawson believes that you should have a varied background. By gaining experience in industry, hospitals, restaurants, and nursing homes, you become aware of procedures in other types of food service operations. Lawson enjoys working in a nursing home. In a restaurant or in industry, you feel isolated from your customers, but this is not true in a nursing home. As Lawson points out, you develop a more personal attitude toward the residents because you have the opportunity to see and talk with them every day. Because of strict state and Federal regulations, you will always be learning. You will learn about food handling, food preparation, sanitation, and safety. You will also become familiar with hospital and institutional fire safety procedures and hazards. It is challenging work to become a licensed food service supervisor. You must start as a cook and gain the necessary experience to rise to head cook and then to supervisor. Each year you will be expected to enroll in continuing education courses to keep up with new developments in nutrition and food service.

## MEDICAL RECORDS TECHNICIAN

You might consider a career as an accredited records technician. With the Federal government requiring more medical records for each patient in a hospital or long-term care facility, there are opportunities for accredited records technicians and registered records administrators. Sometimes these technicians are employed in the admissions department of a nursing home as well as in the administrative department.

In order to be a medical records technician, you must have a knowledge of medical record-keeping procedures and of medicine and medical terms. In addition to working in long-term care facilities, you can work in state health departments, Veterans Administration offices, insurance companies, and acute care hospitals. With a great deal of experience, you can become a consultant to nursing homes that need advice on record-keeping for Medicaid and Medicare patients.

## PSYCHIATRIC HOSPITALS

Besides nursing homes, there are other types of institutional settings where you can work with older adults. County and state mental psychiatric institutions also employ professional and semi-professional employees. If you are employed in this type of institution you will work with patients of all ages; however, there may be separate wards or residences for older adults. Although the number of older adults residing in mental institutions has been reduced in recent years, they still make up a substantial proportion of the population of many county and state mental facilities.

Ramona Nielsen is a supervisor of a senior day center at Marlboro State Hospital in Marlboro, New Jersey. Her task is to orient patients to community life and help them return to the community. Ramona invites guest speakers from the community including representatives from such agencies as Social Security, food stamps, public advocate's office, and the police department to make patients aware of benefits and local programs available to them. She also contacts senior centers and community nutrition programs close to the homes of the patients so that when they return to the community they will have activities in which to participate and to socialize with other older adults. As Ramona points out, "It is important to encourage older adults to use community support systems that are available to all persons in the community. It's important to see that they are not segregated in any way.''

The program at the senior day center is a varied one. It includes various types of therapeutic exercises including music and movement therapy. An occupational therapist helps the members of the center practice daily living skills. A work program coordinator helps members learn vocational skills. All types of skills and hobbies are encouraged, including gardening and farming of small plots by center participants.

Participants are at the half-way stage between institutional living and community living. They are encouraged to plan activities and take trips to community events. They are expected to make choices concerning the daily activities in which they take part. Through a varied program, Ramona and other members of the staff are preparing members of the center to return to the community and participate in daily living activities.

Ramona likes her job and says, ''I am working for my future providing services for older adults.'' Ramona has had previous experience with deinstitutionalization projects—programs for older adults who have spent many years in institutions to reorient them and return them to community living.

## SALARIES FOR INSTITUTIONAL EMPLOYEES

Nursing home administrator salaries vary tremendously according to the size of the facility and whether it is a profit or nonprofit facility. The range of salaries is about $20,000 to $40,000. If the nursing home is part of a religious or charitable order, the administrator may receive a house, a car, or other benefits in addition to agreed-upon salary. Most states have set ceilings on the salary of nursing home administrators. Salaries are also controlled by Medicare and Medicaid formulas, which are related to a base salary plus the number of patient days within a facility. Therefore, the larger the facility, the higher the salary. A normal facility is approximately 120 to 180 beds. In some states there are older and smaller facilities with only 30 to 40 beds. Obviously, salaries in the latter nursing homes are lower.

Recreational therapists with no degree who work as program assistants earn from $8,000 to $12,000 depending upon experience. A senior recreational therapist earns from $11,000 to $15,000. A director of recreational therapy with a large staff could earn $18,000 to $20,000.

Salaries for nurses vary depending on whether they are employed in public facilities as civil service employees or in private nursing homes. Salaries are usually lower in private nursing homes, with a variation of $2,000 to $3,000 less in salary. Licensed practical nurses earn about $11,000 to $12,000 per year. A graduate nurse earns approximately $12,000 to $17,000 per year. A nurse with a bachelor of science degree in nursing would start at least $1,000 higher. A head nurse might earn between $14,000 and $19,000. A supervisor of nursing services could earn between $15,000 and $20,000. A director of nurses in a large convalescent facility could earn between $21,000 and $28,000.

Social workers at the BS entry-level position earn $13,000 to $18,000. A social worker with an MSW could start at $15,000 and earn up to $19,000. Social work supervisors could earn between $16,000 and $21,000.

Physical therapists in acute care hospitals earn between $12,000 and $16,000. However, physical therapists in a large unit who supervise or consult and have their own practice average $22,500. In large cities it is higher. An occupational therapist earns nationally on the average $13,000 to $14,000. However, civil service positions in nursing homes would pay $16,000 on the average for occupational therapists.

A food service supervisor earns between $15,000 and $20,000. A cook starts at approximately $10,000 and rises to $12,000. Many positions such as medical records technician start at $10,000 and rise to $12,000 and $13,000 with many years of experience. A registered records administrator on a national basis earns approximately $18,000 to $19,000 on the average.

Chapter **VII**

# Community Nutrition Programs

The importance to older adults of good food adequately prepared and served in pleasant surroundings was given high priority in recommendations of the White House Conference on Aging in 1971. Throughout the United States, nutrition programs feed large and small numbers of older adults in American Legion halls, firehouses, YMCA's, churches, senior centers, and converted school buildings. In 1980 there were 1,185 nutrition service providers in the U.S. and over 12,500 nutrition sites. The participants at these sites are offered well-balanced meals and companionship, two elements considered primary goals of the program.

In connection with the nutrition program, the Area Agency on Aging develops objectives and monitors and evaluates nutrition service providers. In accomplishing these tasks, the Area Agency also coordinates with the State Agency on Aging. But it is the local nutrition service provider that sponsors and operates the nutrition project day by day.

The project director is responsible for planning, organizing, and administering the nutrition program including delivery of services at each nutrition site. Through a knowledge of community agencies and through delegation of responsibility to skilled personnel, the project director prepares and serves meals for older adults in his area. Although most older adults come to the nutrition site to be served a meal and to socialize with other participants, meals are home-delivered to those who are unable to come to the site either because of illness or handicap.

Many jobs have developed in connection with the expansion of the nutrition program. Some beginning-level jobs require little training or education and provide an opportunity for young people to learn job skills related to working with older adults. Other technical jobs such as project director, food service coordinator, social service coordinator, and accountant require training, education, or professional experience. In general, each nutrition program requires the following positions:

Project Director
Food Service Coordinator
Nutrition Consultant
Social Service Coordinator
Accountant
Site Manager
Cook
Assistant Cook
Food Vehicle Driver
Driver
Dining Room Aide
Outreach Worker
Volunteer Coordinator
Secretary

Jay Zimmer is Assistant Project Director of the Nutrition Project in Ocean County, New Jersey. His duties include developing and supervising the delivery of a variety of social services for older adult participants including transportation, shopping assistance, nutrition education, recreation, and health counseling. He serves as liaison between community groups, the grantee agency, and the project director. One of his most important tasks is to coordinate with site managers regarding participant needs and eligibility for supportive services. He develops training programs for staff and volunteers at the nutrition sites. He assists the director in preparing proposals for grants. He may be called upon to speak to groups on behalf of the project when assigned by the director.

Jay has an interesting background for his job. He attended college in New Hampshire but returned to New Jersey after one year. He obtained a position in the emergency room at Tuxedo Memorial Hospital in Tuxedo, New York. This hospital had a large number of older adult patients, and Jay talked to a lot of them and became concerned about their problems. Many were over seventy-five and worried about being placed in a nursing home. During the two years that he spent at the hospital, Jay was trained as an emergency medical technician and an inhalation therapist. At the same time, he was a student at Ramapo State College in Ramapo, New Jersey.

After graduating with a BS in sociology in June 1974, Jay moved with his family to Toms River and worked in various human service agencies in Ocean County. Early in 1976 Jay noticed an advertisement for a site manager position at a nutrition site in Ocean County. He was hired and later served as social service coordinator before being promoted to assistant project director in January 1980. At twenty-nine Jay has a wide range of responsibilities. He also chairs the Administrator's section of the New Jersey Gerontology Society, a position that helps him to be aware of current issues and trends in the field of aging.

## FOOD SERVICE COORDINATOR

The food service coordinator or nutritionist in a nutrition program has an extremely important position. The person in this position supervises the preparation of all menus, special diets, and related work with the project nutritionist and the project cook. He or she insures that proper sanitary and safety conditions and standards are maintained and inspects all areas where food is received, handled, stored, refrigerated, prepared, and served in a central kitchen and at each nutrition site. The food service coordinator ensures that meals are properly prepared and attractively served to all sites. In addition, he or she is expected to develop and carry out in-service training of staff in food service techniques.

In some projects the food service coordinator is a qualified dietitian who has received training in nutrition and food service in a college degree program. In other projects the project nutritionist or dietitian acts as a consultant who works with the food service coordinator in planning special menus for participants, counseling individual participants on special diets, developing nutrition education materials, and providing in-service training to project staff on nutrition.

## ACCOUNTANT OR BUSINESS MANAGER

Other skilled positions that are required in connection with the operation of the nutrition project include an accountant or business manager. An accounting or business background is necessary to carry out the duties of this position. The accountant is expected to review accounting reports and prepare financial statements. The accountant also prepares budget requests and devises improved accounting methods and recommends their adoption. His day-to-day responsibilities include receiving and checking all bills, preparing checks for payment, and keeping an accurate filing system of all financial records. He is expected to prepare monthly, quarterly, and annual payroll information for submission to the Internal Revenue Service, the State Employment Office, and the State Income Tax Office. One of his most important responsibilities is to keep accurate records on meals and other services that participants receive. The accountant is expected to obtain these statistics from site managers, drivers, outreach workers, and other staff members. Quarterly reports containing these figures are sent to state and national offices on aging. For this position, a bachelor's degree in accounting from an accredited college is required. Usually experience in accounting or auditing operations is expected. Although accounting and food service positions require specialized skills, nevertheless a knowledge of and sensitivity to the needs of older adults is necessary in every position.

## SITE MANAGER

A key position at each site is that of site manager. Each site manager is expected to plan for and supervise a staff that includes volunteers. As manager, he or she must be able to work harmoniously with other staff members, function as a team member, and have some knowledge of agencies and resources available to the elderly in the community.

Although they work only 25 or 30 hours a week, they are busy from the time they arrive at the nutrition site until the time they leave. They interview project participants to obtain necessary information for record-keeping purposes. They are responsible for maintaining food service records and files. They establish work schedules for the staff and assist in the training of personnel.

Each nutrition site develops a personality of its own. This depends on the people who come to the site and the nature of the community surrounding it. But it is the site manager who sets the tone and atmosphere. The site manager becomes familiar with everyone coming to the nutrition site. The participants come to know and trust the site manager. Very often they confide their most personal problems to the site manager who greets them and talks with them each day.

If you would like to become a site manager, you should have experience in direct services or health services for the elderly. You should be sensitive to the needs of older adults and be able to relate to them in a manner that maintains and fosters their dignity. If you can deal with the problems of managing a large staff that includes volunteers and be concerned about the elderly participants who come to the nutrition site every day, perhaps you can qualify for the important job of site manager.

## MEALS ON WHEELS PROGRAMS

In addition to meals that are served at nutrition sites in group fashion, there are also individual nutrition services for shut-ins or elderly persons who are disabled or convalescent and have difficulty shopping and preparing meals. Some older adults also lack facilities for preparing well-balanced meals or are so lonely that they have little desire to do so. These services are usually called meals on wheels or mobile meals projects. Some are associated with nutrition service providers and others are independent.

Meals on wheels programs provide an opportunity for socialization as well as nutrition.

Mobile Meals of Monmouth County, Incorporated delivers hot nutritious meals to older adults in various communities in Monmouth County, New Jersey. Barbara Frink is the Director. Her duties include supervising a staff that includes an assistant and two program aides. She interviews applicants for the project to determine their eligibility and dietary needs. Each day she maintains contact with the facilities that supply the meals and informs them of the dietary needs of each participant. She also maintains communication with the applicants' physician, with community nursing services, and other agencies that provide services to participants. Barbara delivers meals in emergencies and observes and evaluates the quality of the meals prepared by the various facilities.

Barbara believes that mobile meals is an alternative to a participant's going into a nursing home. The program helps relieve the isolation and loneliness of the older person. The program usually coordinates with other community programs serving the elderly. Barbara often sees the results of her efforts, and as a result she thoroughly enjoys her position.

Of course, there are disadvantages to every job. Sometimes it is difficult to help some of the participants. They neglect their health and nutrition in order to pay utility bills or taxes to keep their home or residence. Mobile meals is primarily a volunteer operation. Both staff and facilities volunteer to provide services to participants. Therefore, as a staff member you must be diplomatic in informing them of mistakes in food service or in delivery of meals.

But every Monday through Friday (and holidays also), volunteers deliver meals to shut-ins and convalescents. There are 200 regular volunteers and 400 temporary volunteers who sign up as substitutes to be called from time to time. In 1980 over 36,000 meals were delivered to elderly participants in Monmouth County.

How did Barbara obtain her present position? She was a secretary for three years at Fort Monmouth, an army installation near Red Bank, New Jersey. After a ten-year break as a homemaker, raising a family, she decided to return to the job market. She worked in a preschool program at Fort Monmouth for one year and then applied for her present position. One of the reasons she was chosen over the other applicants was that she had experience as a volunteer in a mobile meals program. In 1975 Barbara saw an article concerning volunteering in community activities. As a result she became a mobile meals volunteer for two years. She has also taken courses in gerontology at the local community college.

Barbara feels that three things are necessary to carry out the responsibilities of a mobile meals program. You should have a basic business background, a human services background, and a general knowledge of food services and nutrition. At times you will need to put yourself in the place of a participant and try to understand his or her problems. This can leave you very frustrated. As Barbara says, you must concentrate on your satisfactions or what you can do for the participant rather than on your disappointments or what you cannot accomplish.

Socialization at an Ocean City nutrition center culminated in wedding bells for these older adults.

## COOK

In a nutrition project, the cook is charged with planning, coordinating, and timing the work in the kitchen so that meals are ready for serving to participants without overcooking or waste. Since cooking for a nutrition project involves preparing hundreds of meals, quantity cooking procedures must be used in preparing meats, poultry, fish, sauces, and gravies. In addition to preparing food in an appealing and acceptable manner, the cook insures that proper sanitation and safety procedures are carried out and work areas are kept neat and clean. An important task for the cook and his or her staff is to portion food correctly for serving and measure and weigh portions and ingredients as required.

Physical effort required in kitchen management is strenuous. Cooks often lift and move objects of over 30 pounds and occasionally over 50 pounds. Experience for this job can be obtained through previous responsibility in kitchen management, through on-the-job training, and by taking prescribed food management and food sanitation courses in vocational-technical schools or community colleges.

Older adults have had years of experience in preparing and cooking food and at times will be critical of quantity cooking methods. Sometimes salt must be kept to a minimum because of dietary restrictions. In some nutrition projects, a knowledge of local ethnic eating tastes or recipes is required. In areas of predominantly Jewish population, a knowledge of kosher dietary laws is necessary.

If you decide to become a cook at a nutrition project, your job will be challenging as you strive to meet the needs and widely varying tastes of older adults that you will be serving.

## MISCELLANEOUS JOBS

There are positions that require less skill and involve smaller salary. These positions include relief or assistant site manager. This job enables a project director to determine if an employee has the ability to relate well to other employees and to manage a nutrition site. The relief site manager is on call and performs the duties of a site manager in case of absence or illness of the regular manager. Usually the relief site manager is a trouble shooter and may be sent from one site to another when absences occur.

Other positions include kitchen or dining room aide. This may be a staff or volunteer position. There are many older adults who willingly perform this task and serve their fellow participants. At some nutrition projects, the dining room aide may be involved in outreach functions, in which case they are called outreach workers and make outreach and follow-up calls on participants as directed by the site manager.

The main function of an outreach worker is identifying participants for the nutrition project through door-to-door canvassing, telephone contact, or referral from other agencies. Outreach are employed part time are paid an hourly rate. Social service coordinators earn between $12,000 and $16,000. However, these services are often contracted out to a private agency at an agreed-upon rate. In some cases, site managers are employed on an hourly basis and earn only minimum wages, approximately $3 to $4 per hour. In other projects, site managers must take a civil service test, and they earn between $9,000 and $12,000. Cooks are paid approximately the same salary. An accountant in a nutrition project earns between $12,000 and $18,000. Mobile meals or meals on wheels coordinators may earn only $6,000 to $7,000 if employed part time. If employed full time they earn about $12,000 to $15,000. Drivers earn between $7,000 and $9,500, intake and outreach workers about $7,000. Dining room aides are often employed from public service projects and receive minimum wages of $3.35 per hour. Other part-time employees also receive the minimum wage.

workers arrange for transportation to nutrition sit
areas, medical facilities, and social service agencies wh
They make follow-up contacts when hard-to-reach
discontinue attendance at a nutrition site.

In general, outreach workers at a nutrition site m
communication skills. They must have a knowledge of
ty to the needs of older adults. They are expected to w
staff members and volunteers at the site. In many
operate on their own and must have a good driving

Drivers are important team members of a nutri
They provide transportation for eligible participant
the nutrition site. They assist participants into and o
needed, always assuring their maximum comfort a
ensure that the vehicle is maintained in good conditic
meals to participants who are temporarily hon
should have reasonably good health and strength
heavy lifting. As drivers, they must have a licen
physical or mental defect that would affect their ab
motor vehicle.

## SALARIES AND WAGES FOR NUTRITION :
## PROVIDERS

As nutrition projects have expanded in size, s
have increased. As an employee of a nutrition ser
will not become rich. On the other hand, you sh
paid a salary commensurate with your training a
salaries given are subject to variation dependin
project sponsor is a private business, a nonprofi
civil service salary ranges on the local, county, c

The highest salaried person is the project direc
highly developed management and human relat
range from $18,000 to $28,000, higher in a large
service coordinators earn between $17,000 and $

*Chapter* **VIII**

---

# Teaching and Learning About Older Adults

How would you like to teach older adults? Those of you who have considered becoming a teacher have probably thought about teaching an elementary, junior high school, or senior high school class. But have you considered teaching a retired group of older adults? Can you imagine what it would be like to teach someone with a lifetime of experience, one who is seventy, eighty, or even ninety years old? Rick Moody, an instructor for the Institute of Study for Older Adults at the New York City Technical College, states, "To go into the presence of an eighty- or ninety-year-old student when your previous experience has been teaching at the secondary level is a tremendous experience. There is an extraordinary richness of life experience in these students who describe what it was like to be attacked by Cossacks in Russia or to grow up in the lemon groves of Sicily before emigrating to America many years ago."

Perhaps what teachers like about students who are older adults is that they are not compelled to come to class. They come because they want to learn. They come to class because they would rather learn than remain at home and knit or watch television.

Rick, who has ten years' experience teaching older adults, points out that the job of educators is to challenge the older adult.

Rick has used stories about the culture of the native country of the older adult as a method of teaching. While their enthusiasm and willingness to learn are a definite advantage, there are disadvantages in teaching older adults. Rick says that they often rely on their own life experience and seldom accept other points of view or change their opinion on issues brought up in class. Because of their age, sometimes they may become ill or die during the term in which the instructor is teaching them.

Are there opportunities in teaching older adults at the present time? Rick Moody says, "There has to be a future in teaching older adults." However, at the present time, funds for educational programs for older adults are limited. There are part-time teaching opportunities for graduate students, retired teachers, and professionals who cannot follow an educational career full time. Other professionals such as artists, actors, or musicians who may have some free time can find part-time instruction teaching older adults. Part-time instructors in the New York area were receiving $18 to $20 per hour to teach older adults in 1980. This salary serves to demonstrate that you will not become rich teaching older adults.

Programs for older adults are expanding in senior centers, nutrition sites, and other community locations where seniors meet. Edith Smith is educational program supervisor for the Waxter Senior Center in Baltimore. The courses at the center help the participants meet one another, increase communication and learning, and improve their ability to serve in their communities. Many courses are offered for the 700 older adults who come to Waxter each day. Courses to improve creativity include sewing, needlework, sculpture, ceramics, painting, weaving, print-making, and quilting. Other courses include adult basic education (learning to read and write) and language classes such as French, German, Italian, and Spanish. Writing, history, and foreign policy are other courses that are of interest to older adults.

Edith's philosophy is simple and practical: In preparing educational programs for older students, find out what courses they want. Edith emphasizes that the training for teachers of older adults is no different than for younger students. A knowledge of gerontology will be helpful, but good teaching is necessary no matter what the age level of the students.

Edith has a varied background in teaching and supervising educational programs. She started as an elementary teacher, then became involved in adult education and in 1970 joined the education division of Activities for Golden Age, a human services agency in Baltimore. In 1974 she joined Waxter as Director of Education. She has over eleven years of teaching and program planning experience with older adults.

COURTESY OCEAN COUNTY COMMUNITY COLLEGE

Students in a gerontology class.

Edith enjoys working with the instructors in art appreciation classes. She helps schedule visits for students to art galleries in the Baltimore and Washington area. Seniors seem to become more critical of their own art work after visiting art museums. She also helps in planning educational activities for the physically or mentally handicapped senior. Often basic craft activities are of interest to them. One of the courses that Edith feels is of great benefit to students and is one of the most popular at Waxter is adult basic education. Here seniors are realizing a lifelong ambition by learning to read and write. According to Edith, class participants become more assertive and more confident when they complete the course.

How can you obtain experience or training to teach older adults? You might volunteer to teach part time at a senior center or a nutrition site in a subject or craft in which you have some skill. You could start as a program assistant and develop or assist in planning programs for older adults at a senior center. As part of your college coursework, you could participate in internships or field work that would include visits to retirement housing complexes, nutrition sites, or senior centers.

In addition to the large number of organizations and agencies offering educational programs for the well elderly, there are a number of colleges and secondary schools that provide educational instruction for the homebound elderly. The New York Technical College program is an example. Senior companions are hired to perform part-time teaching of older adults. Television programs are used as the main source of instruction. Each week discussion questions are prepared by instructors for the senior companions, who will use them with the homebound student. Questions and answers given by the homebound student are then brought back to classes that are attended by the senior companions. These classes provide feedback concerning what topics are of the greatest interest to the homebound student.

Joan Delaloye is the coordinator of this program. According to Joan, to be successful in supervising an educational program for older adults you need many skills. You need organizational skills, communication skills, writing skills, and record-keeping skills. You also need patience and enthusiasm to encourage older adults to want to learn. Even if they are ill or disabled, you can help them continue to learn. Joan points out that the program is important for older adults because the senior companions treat them as someone capable of learning rather than as a frail homebound patient.

Joan started as a caseworker for a child welfare agency after graduating from St. John's University in Brooklyn, New York, in 1967. As a caseworker Joan learned to identify resources in the community. After eight years she went back to school, and she graduated from the Fordham University School of Social Work with a master's degree in social work. In 1978 Joan started as a student intern at the Institute of Study for Older Adults. Later she became coordinator of the program, which is described as extending continuing education to the elderly homebound. In reviewing her job experience and graduate education, Joan feels that first obtaining work experience and then completing graduate school was very helpful. Her previous social work background helps her in achieving the cooperation of other agencies as coordinator. Among her duties, she interviews instructors for the program, she works with an advisory committee that includes representatives from television and other media, and she informs other agencies of the programs of the Institute of Study for Older Adults.

For students considering a career in educating older adults, Joan recommends obtaining experience by volunteering in nursing homes or senior centers. According to Joan, working with older adults is stimulating because many have had little education and they want to share their life experience with others. There are disadvantages also in teaching older adults. You must allow them to proceed at their own pace. Sometimes this means that you as a teacher or a supervisor will have to modify your expectations or reduce the amount of material that you expect them to learn. Second, programs for the education of the homebound elderly are often started with Federal funds, and these funds may be reduced or stopped. Sometimes instructors and supervisors such as Joan, after encouraging older adults to continue learning, have to discontinue classes or programs because of lack of funds.

## GERONTOLOGY: TEACHING AND LEARNING ABOUT OLDER ADULTS

Perhaps you would rather be involved in encouraging older students to learn about older adults. Many schools and colleges are expanding programs for students who are interested in gerontology, or the science of learning about older adults.

Judy Donini is an instructor in sociology and gerontology at Ocean County College, Toms River, New Jersey. Judy finds it challenging to teach gerontology. "I like educating people who have misconceptions about the elderly. Most of my students are interested in understanding older adults because of their contact with someone in their family."

Participants help each other in activity programs at senior centers.

Like many other students of gerontology, Judy became interested in the field through a course in college. At Trenton State College, Judy registered for a course in adult development and aging. A class requirement was spending six hours per week in contact with well elderly people in retirement housing, nutrition sites, and other areas where older adults congregated. After receiving a degree in psychology from Trenton State in 1976, Judy searched for a university where she could pursue a graduate program in gerontology. She identified the University of South Florida at Tampa as a resource center for the study of death and dying. For that reason, she enrolled in the graduate program in gerontology and graduated in 1977. During her graduate work, she spent six months as an intern at the Princeton Senior Resource Center in Princeton, New Jersey. Following graduation, she was employed as a social service designee at Meadow Lakes, a skilled nursing home facility in Hightstown, New Jersey. She interviewed residents concerning their social history, performed patient counseling, and attended patient conferences with social workers, psychologists, nurses, doctors, and other professionals at the facility. As a recent graduate in gerontology, she found the job challenging and a positive experience.

In August 1979 she was hired as an instructor in sociology and gerontology to develop a program in gerontology at the community college level. Judy has been teaching for two years at Ocean County Community College. She teaches the courses Introduction to Gerontology and Sociology of Aging. Aside from preparing for her classes and contact with her students, Judy is associate editor of the *New Jersey Gerontological Society Bulletin* and is treasurer of the New Jersey Sociological Society. During the summer months, Judy is enrolled at Trenton State College in courses concerned with counseling of older adults. At the age of twenty-seven, Judy is continually learning more about her chosen field of gerontology.

## *GERONTOLOGICAL NURSING EDUCATOR*

There are a number of professions that are concerned with providing care for older adults. Perhaps none is more important than the nursing profession. For those nurses who have received their nursing education and want to specialize in helping older adults, the gerontological nurse practitioner is in demand.

Linda Janelli is employed as coordinator of a gerontological nurse practitioner program at Niagara University, Niagara, New York. The way Linda became involved in nursing education concerning older adults is roundabout, and yet it shows the type of training that most young nurses must obtain if they are to become employed in helping older adults.

Linda's education was varied and lengthy. She attended Cooper Hospital in Camden, New Jersey, as a student in a three-year nursing program. Following graduation in 1969, she worked in the intensive care ward at Atlantic City Medical Center in Atlantic City, New Jersey, during 1970 and 1971. In 1971 she volunteered for service in the Air Force and was stationed as an Air Force lieutenant in California. Later she became a flight nurse and traveled between the Philippines and California air bases transporting wounded service personnel and former prisoners of war from Vietnam. After two years in the Air Force, she was discharged but remained in the Air Force Reserve and aided in the evacuation of refugees from Vietnam. At present she is a captain in the Air Force Reserve.

After discharge from the Air Force, Linda continued her education in California, enrolling in a community college in Fairfield, and in 1973 she graduated with an associate in arts degree. Returning to New Jersey, she learned of a program for graduate nurses at Stockton State College in Pomona through which she could obtain a bachelor's degree in nursing. As part of her coursework at Stockton, Linda participated in a health services survey for older adults in the Atlantic City area. She visited nutrition sites and senior centers and through interviews with older adults identified the kind of health care services they needed. As a result, Linda became interested in working with older adults and applied for a job in a clinic for the well elderly located in Atlantic City. Her duties included performing nursing assessments of older people and providing health instruction to groups of older people. During the summer of 1978 she learned of a master's program in primary health care for the aged that was offered at Seton Hall University in South Orange, New Jersey. She applied for and was accepted in this program, and in September 1979 she graduated with a master's degree in gerontological nursing.

Upon graduation, she became Assistant Director of Preakness Hospital in Wayne, New Jersey. There Linda was involved in patient care and staff development at a 380-bed long-term care facility. In November 1980, Linda saw an advertisement in the *American Journal of Nursing* for a gerontological nurse to assist in identifying nursing concepts concerned with older adult patients in an undergraduate nursing curriculum. The position was at Niagara University in Niagara, New York, and she was hired for it in January 1981.

How did Linda obtain her job in gerontological nursing? First, she had over ten years of increasingly responsible experience combined with graduate education. Her experience was varied and interspersed with continuous education. In her present position, she is coordinator of the nursing curriculum project and assists the director in curriculum development. She also acts as an adjunct instructor and uses role-playing and simulation games to teach student nurses in her classes. Other tasks include assisting in the writing of grant proposals to the Federal government, and reviewing films and videotapes for possible use in the nursing curriculum. She also enjoys attending conferences in gerontological nursing and meeting stimulating professional educators who come to Niagara University. Recently Linda reviewed a new book entitled *Gerontological Instruction in Higher Education* for the *Journal of Gerontological Nursing.* In all of these tasks, she is making use of her experience and training received in New Jersey and in the Armed Forces.

For a nurse with acute care experience, there are disadvantages to becoming a nursing educator. As Linda points out, teaching does not involve as much feedback from patients as you would obtain in a primary care facility or hospital. Sometimes Linda finds her new duties frustrating and quite different from her previous role as a nurse. Yet she feels that her education has helped prepare her for this position. Her graduate work educated her in health deviations of older adults, in acting as a supporter of health measures for older adults, and in performing nursing research. Linda states, "Too often nurses are not educated to perform research, and they are dependent on sociologists and psychologists to provide the nursing profession with knowledge." Linda Janelli at the age of thirty-two is well trained to move ahead in her chosen field of gerontological nursing.

## LIBRARY SERVICES FOR THE AGED

Are there other positions involving education where you are concerned with helping older adults to learn or helping individuals who work with older adults to increase their knowledge? Allan Kleiman believes there is another career where you can serve older adults and help professional people who are interested in learning about older adults.

Allan is a professional librarian and director of SAGE—Services for the Aging—at the Kings Highway Branch of the Brooklyn Public Library. The program provides specialized services to older adults including Book Talks (describing the contents of a book to a small group of library customers), large-print books, talking book services (for older adults who have visual handicaps), and mail services for library patrons who have difficulty getting to the library. Other programs include books and films concerned with the cultural background of countries from which older adults emigrated. Of course, some older adults enjoy the best sellers like any other library patron, but others enjoy and welcome the special programs offered by the Brooklyn Public Library.

Because there is a large concentration of senior citizens in Brooklyn—over 270,000—there is a need for specialized services for them. These services include providing book and film delivery to senior centers and nursing homes throughout the borough. In addition, trained senior assistants have been placed in each of the fifteen branch libraries to help schedule film programs, secure outside speakers, and organize special music and dance programs for older adults. About half of these senior assistants provide programs in nursing homes and senior centers near the branch library.

How do you become involved in helping older adults as a librarian? First and most important, you should become a professional librarian. Perhaps Allan's experience will illustrate the kind of experience or training that is necessary.

Allan Kleiman started working in the Brooklyn Public Library when he was sixteen as a clerk shelving books. He left the library during college to make more money in retailing. However, after graduating from Brooklyn College in 1973 and St. John's University in 1974, from which he received a master's degree in library science, he returned to the Brooklyn Public Library. As soon as he was hired as a librarian in 1974, he found himself planning activities for older adults who came to the library during the afternoons. While Allan worked in the Canarsie branch of the Library, he assisted senior companions in choosing library materials for the homebound elderly. These senior companions worked for social service agencies and visited shut-ins and homebound elderly clients. He also became a member of the InterAgency Council, where he was involved in planning and recommending library services for older adults. He became active in the American Library Association and served on committees concerned with providing library services to the older population. Slowly, through voluntary effort and as part of his job, Allan became knowledgeable about library programs for older adults.

When the previous director moved on to another job, Allan was asked to become the director of the SAGE program for the Brooklyn Public Library. Currently he is enrolled in a doctoral program in library science at Columbia University and is planning to make a survey of library services available for older adults throughout the United States for his thesis topic. He also serves as a library representative on numerous committees concerned with providing services to the aging in the city of New York.

If you are to succeed as a librarian serving older adults, Allan emphasizes that you must choose programs of interest to the age group. You must be sure that each program is brief and on the educational level of the participants. You should try to present programs concerned with their cultural background. You should also be sure that you can provide large-print books, mail services, and talking-book services for your older adult patrons.

In addition, Allan believes that good public relations are needed to serve an older adult clientele. Too often libraries don't get enough publicity about the programs and services they offer to the public.

Allan says, "A good knowledge of organizations serving older adults will help librarians piggyback library services to older adults." At thirty, Allan has developed a wide background of experience serving the older population of Brooklyn.

While library service to the elderly is a relatively new field, such specialized services will continue to expand in coming years. You might be interested in obtaining experience either as a volunteer or student intern in a library where there is a large number of older adult patrons. In a short time you will learn of their needs and desires. You would be advised to obtain graduate library training and then obtain on-the-job experience or specialized training to serve older adults who will be coming to libraries in increasing numbers.

## SALARIES IN TEACHING AND LEARNING ABOUT OLDER ADULTS

As a teacher of older adults you certainly will not get rich at the present time. There are many part-time teaching jobs in which you will be paid on an hourly basis. Salaries range from $5 to $15 per hour. As a program director or educational director at a senior center in a large city, you would earn $15,000 to $20,000. College faculty salaries vary tremendously from South to North and from large cities to small towns. An instructor would earn between $11,000 and $15,000. A faculty member with nursing background would obviously earn more. Depending upon the rank, either instructor, assistant or associate professor, a gerontological nurse practitioner would earn between $17,000 and $24,000; in large cities add $5,000. Librarians with a master's degree would earn between $15,000 and $20,000 and rise to higher salaries in large cities in supervisory positions.

*Chapter* **IX**

---

# Working in a Hospice

If you are to seek a job or vocation involved with older adults, perhaps you would be interested in working in or volunteering your services in a hospice program. Hospice comes from the Latin word meaning host or receiver. Webster defines hospice as a place of shelter maintained by monks or a home for the sick or poor. In medieval times, hospices were places where monks provided rest for travelers on long and difficult journeys. During the nineteenth century, the Sisters of Charity, a Catholic religious order, developed hospices in Ireland as a place for the dying—those who were terminally ill or infirm and whose family did not have the space, time, energy, or skill to care for them properly. The Irish nuns provided a place where a dying person could be brought for loving care.

The American model of a hospice owes much to the concept of care started by Dr. Cicely Saunders in Sydenham, England, in 1967 called Saint Christopher's hospice. Many American health care officials have visited Saint Christopher's to observe and study the methods used. Dr. Saunders realized that many patients were receiving inadequate care in hospitals and that relatives were having problems caring for the dying person at home. She started a program in which patients who knew their death was imminent could enter the program and receive appropriate pain control during their illness. The program provided a wide variety of services including medical, nursing, psychological, and religious services. Family support and counseling services after the death of the patient were included as part of the program.

The objectives of most hospices in the United States include assisting the patient and his family to participate in the patient's health care, offering an alternative to placing the patient in a hospital or nursing home, and helping to control pain through adequate medication.

Upon what basis are patients admitted to a hospice program? Since many hospices are located in or near a hospital, many hospices limit patient acceptance to the residence area served by a hospital. Other requirements include prognosis of life expectancy measured in weeks or months, someone who is willing to care for the patient at home, active participation by the patient's physician in the hospice program, and admission regardless of the patient's ability to pay.

The beginning of the Raritan Bay Health Services Corporation Hospice in Perth Amboy, New Jersey, demonstrates how hospice programs are started. Edna Seyffart, a registered nurse, is director of the program. Edna was supervisor of acute care at Raritan Bay Health Services Corporation based in Perth Amboy General Hospital. As supervisor she often used crisis intervention methods— talking with and counseling family members who brought a relative to the acute care section during a terminal illness. In 1977 she attended a lecture by Dr. Elizabeth Kubler Ross, a noted author, on the subject of death and dying. After hearing the lecture, Edna was motivated to start a hospice program. First, she performed a feasibility study at Perth Amboy General Hospital to determine how many patients who had died during the previous year could have benefited from a hospice program. She found that over 140 patients could have benefited from such a program. In 1978 Edna and her husband traveled to England and visited Saint Christopher's hospice near London. Upon returning, Edna started a program for five patients during her off-duty hours with the encouragement of Mary Konyk, chairperson of nursing services at the hospital, and the support of the Raritan Bay Health Services Corporation. In 1979 through a grant from the United Way Fund of Central New Jersey, Edna was released from her duties as supervisor to coordinate the hospice program.

In order to raise funds and educate the community about the hospice program, Edna and Ray Gebauer, a teacher and an audiovisual coordinator, developed an audiovisual slide presentation describing the work carried on by the hospice program. Edna told the story of Monk Watson, a former vaudeville magician, who was dying of cancer. He was shown being cared for at home and demonstrating card tricks to friends and volunteers who came to visit him. By taking the slide presentation to church groups, adult education classes, and community service organizations such as the Lions and Elks, Edna helped inform and educate community groups about the hospice program.

In the slide presentation, Edna stated, "We believe that an individual facing death is entitled to live the last days meaningfully in dignity and in peace. Because of this our staff assists in maintaining the patient in the comfort of his own home."

Where are hospices located? In 1981 there were over 200 hospices throughout the United States. They may be in the form of hospital-based units, free-standing facilities or expanded home care services. Although many hospices are associated with hospitals, the hospice program is a separate and distinct unit. If the hospice is free-standing, it is housed in a separate building or facility within the community. Professionals whose services are needed are drawn from the community and become part of the hospice staff on a full- or part-time basis. Other hospice programs may concentrate on the expansion of home care services and be associated with community health care or visiting nurse associations. In all hospice programs, the emphasis is on the patient and his family or primary care person as the location of care.

An important part of the hospice program is the primary care person. Often this is a daughter of the patient or a neighbor or a paid professional. If the patient's family cannot provide care, then the hospice staff will provide backup support or training and education for the family of the patient. This support may include the services of a chaplain, psychologist, social worker, physical therapist, or a home care nurse twenty-four hours a day.

If you were to work in a hospice, what sort of professional training should you have? In general, the staff of a hospice includes health care professionals, particularly someone who has had community nursing experience. A social worker and a secretary would also be required for a small hospice. However, large hospices are staffed with a complete range of health care professionals, including a physician, an internist, a surgeon, an administrator, a mental health consultant or psychologist, a psychiatrist, a chaplain,

COURTESY RARITAN BAY HEALTH SERVICES CORPORATION HOSPICE
Members of a hospice staff counsel a member of a patient's family.

a dietitian, a pharmacist, and a physical therapist. A nursing coordinator and various types of nursing specialists including nurse's aides would also be on the staff. In some hospice programs, art therapists and music therapists are employed as specialists to help patients explore their feelings during the last stage of their life. At the Riverside Hospice in Boonton, New Jersey, a bereavement coordinator was employed. Normally the person hired for this position is required to have a strong background in family counseling or casework and experience as a social worker. The duties include counseling the patient's family after the bereavement at specific time intervals—one month, three months, six months, and one year. The bereavement coordinator trains staff and supervises volunteers to insure that visits to the family are carried out. If you expect to become employed in a hospice program, you will need to be a highly trained and motivated health care individual.

Most hospice programs emphasize the importance of supporting and counseling the patient's family after the bereavement. This counseling may include family life groups that bring together a small number of patient families who share experiences concerned with death and dying. One person who has experienced grief in the past six months is more likely to be able to support and comfort someone whose loved one has just died. In some hospice programs there are groups for children with a family member who is a terminal patient.

An important part of the hospice team is the social worker. According to Gwen Smith, a social worker at the Riverview Hospice in Red Bank, New Jersey, social workers on a hospice team should have experience in providing concrete services to patients and their families. They should be familiar with services such as Social Security, Medicaid and Medicare regulations, food stamp requirements, and services provided by mental health clinics. They should believe in the importance of continuity of care for the family from the time the patient enters the hospital until the time of death and one year after. Often social workers and other staff members attend wakes and funerals as part of their responsibilities.

One of the important tasks of the social worker, according to Gwen, is to explain the philosophy of hospice care to the patient and his family. The hospice program does not place great emphasis on life-support systems such as chemotherapy, radiology, and other approaches to cure the patient, but is rather a method to help the patient remain comfortable while dealing with the process of dying and probable death. Sometimes there is conflict between the patient and the family. The patient may wish to die and the patient's family may want further efforts made to prolong his or her life. Overall, the hospice philosophy is to try to meet the needs of the patient. The acceptance of the hospice program is not a permanent decision for the patient; he may change his mind and decide on strong health care measures to prolong life.

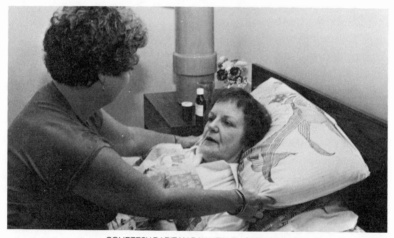

COURTESY RARITAN BAY HEALTH SERVICES CORPORATION HOSPICE
A volunteer visits a hospice patient.

Perhaps the most important function of the social worker is to promote communication between the patient and the family. At all times the social worker tries to focus on day-to-day living experiences of the patient. She assists the patient in maintaining contact with friends and helps contact outside organizations when necessary.

In order to carry out her responsibilities as a social worker in a hospice program, Gwen Smith has a wide background of experience including work in a mental health clinic, in direct service counseling with a county welfare agency, and as an intern in a family and children's health clinic. Gwen's education and training include a bachelor's degree in social work from Kean College in Union, New Jersey, and a master's degree in social work from Rutgers University in New Brunswick, New Jersey. This training and education help provide Gwen with the background necessary to counsel hospice patients and their families.

## ADVANTAGES IN WORKING IN A HOSPICE PROGRAM

If you are interested in working in a hospice program, the demand for trained personnel in this field is increasing. The number of hospices has expanded since 1975. The National Hospice Association in McLean, Virginia, provides education and training opportunities for personnel employed in hospices.

Ginny Sullivan, a registered nurse, is employed at the Raritan Bay Health Services Corporation Hospice in Perth Amboy, New Jersey. She believes there are advantages for a professional nurse who works in a hospice program. The hospice nurse is trained to assist families and help patients during terminal illness. In addition to their professional responsibilities, they are often involved in the ordinary decisions that every dying person must make—what funeral director will be requested, what color dress, what color suit the patient wishes to wear, and whether there will be a day or evening viewing. The hours are more flexible for a staff nurse in a hospice program than in an acute care facility. In a hospital or acute care facility a nurse may be involved in shift work or continuous night and weekend duty depending upon her assigned schedule. While the hospice team member does make home visits during evenings and weekends, the responsibilities are less intensive.

However, Ginny points out that you must be flexible as far as your working hours are concerned. You cannot expect to work a nine-to-five schedule each week. Often you will be called to assist a patient at home or to visit with the family during a crisis in the patient's illness or death. You cannot be a highly structured person. You will not always be able to leave your office at a fixed time. If you have a family, your family should be aware of your overtime responsibilities.

What sort of personality do you need if you are to work in a hospice program? At the Raritan Bay Health Services Corporation Hospice, each staff member finds time to express a sense of humor. Because staff members are often involved in crisis situations, they must have the ability to laugh and joke with one another over day-to-day occurrences. If you are to work as a team member in a hospice, you should have this ability.

What are the disadvantages of working in a hospice program? The first and most obvious disadvantage is that most if not all of your patients will die, and you as a hospice staff member must help the family and the patient accept this. Second, staff burnout can occur. Staff members of a hospice program may become depressed or lack the desire to continue in the program and carry out their responsibilities. Third, as a hospice team member you will become very familiar with the families of your patients. These families may become dependent upon you, particularly after the bereavement. Of course, most hospice teams have methods of dealing with this problem. They may have weekly group counseling sessions in which they can share feelings about patients and families with whom they are working daily. At the Raritan Bay Hospice, the staff meets twice a month to discuss such problems with a trained counselor.

How can you learn whether you have the temperament and personality to become a staff member of a hospice team? You can obtain some training as a volunteer. Most hospice programs have emphasized continuous volunteer training. Staff members are willing to take time to train volunteers because they are an important part of the program. As a volunteer you would participate as a member of a hospice team and visit the patient and the patient's family. It is not an easy task, but as Edna Seyffart, director of the Raritan Bay Health Services Corporation Hospice, points out,

"Death is a normal process through which all must pass. The beauty of death is evident in the fall as leaves turn color and die and adorn the trees in all their splendor. These shortly fall to the ground and lie amidst the grass, soon to be absorbed into the balance of nature."

## SALARIES FOR HOSPICE STAFF

Salaries for health care personnel have been described in other chapters. However, if a director of a hospice were a nurse she would earn approximately $18,000 to $22,000. In a large city the salary would be $22,000 to $25,000.

*Chapter* **X**

# Federal, State, and Local Government Jobs

All of the jobs mentioned in this chapter are challenging and rewarding, and if you decide on such a career in government you will certainly be doing useful work for others and for society. You will find that you will be able to use all the education and training you have acquired. Of course, each government agency is different and has different goals. As a government employee you will be part of a large organization, but you may work in a smaller district or branch office in a state or region. If you decide upon a career as a government employee, you will learn that your fellow workers share your background and ability and you can depend upon them for advice and information when you begin.

Only a few government agencies and positions can be described in this chapter. Those that are mentioned deal with large numbers of older adults in addition to other age groups. One of these agencies is the Social Security Administration. Offices of the Social Security Administration are spread throughout the country in almost 1,300 field offices and six program centers. About two-thirds of the 75,000 employees of the Social Security Administration work in local offices. A local office requires service representatives and claims representatives in addition to other management, secretarial, and clerical positions. If you like to work with people you may be interested in the kind of work performed in these positions. You will need to be familiar with all aspects of social security laws and regulations. You will deal with retirement, survivors, disability, and health insurance benefits. You will be concerned with programs for the aged, the blind, and the disabled under the Supplemental Security Income Program. You will have to keep up with the changes and amendments to Social Security laws as they are passed by the Congress of the United States.

As a claims representative in a Social Security office you will take applications for all types of Social Security benefits including supplemental security income, disability, and other programs for all age groups. You will also be expected to answer basic questions concerning benefits and programs. As a service representative you will be responsible for all types of post-entitlement benefits, including Medicare and other programs.

John Guarascio is a field representative for the Social Security Administration district office in Asbury Park, New Jersey. In his job he is involved in public relations activities. He speaks to service clubs and community organizations and discusses general information about Social Security programs. For other groups, such as medical associations or hospital administrators, he speaks on more specific programs or benefits including changes in Medicare or kidney dialysis treatment benefits. As part of his responsibilities, he visits older adults who are homebound or live in nursing homes or boarding homes and discusses Social Security benefits with them. John meets and talks with all types of older adults in the community.

John says, "As a Social Security employee, you represent the Federal government. In many cases, you are the first person employed by a government agency to have any contact with an older person. In dealing with older adults, you must be fair and yet be a caring person. You will fill out forms and take applications concerning Social Security benefits. But you will also listen to older people talk about their life and what they have accomplished." One older person told John of competing with Johnny Weismuller, one of the first actors to play Tarzan in a motion picture, in the 1928 Olympics swimming events. You will find that each applicant is different and unique.

John Guarascio's background is similar to those of many employees in the Social Security Administration. He started as a service representative and advanced to more responsible positions. He started as a GS-4 employee with the New Rochelle, New York, district office in 1969. While obtaining a college degree, he moved to various Social Security offices and gained more experience and training. In 1972 he received a bachelor's degree in psychology and sociology from Manhattan College in New York City. During this period he worked as a claims representative in White Plains, New York, and then transferred to district offices in the New Jersey shore area, where he was given more varied responsibilities. At thirty-five John is a field representative at the GS-10 level with over twelve years' experience with the Social Security Administration.

FACE TO FACE—Social Security Representative John A. Guarascio is shown interviewing a potential social security recipient.

One of the advantages of being employed by the Social Security Administration is that you can transfer from one part of the country to another. If you want to work in California or Alaska, you can apply for a position in one of those states when there are openings. You may not receive a promotion every time you decide to transfer, but you will have the opportunity to live and work in various parts of the country.

Rosemary Jamrozy is an operations supervisor in the Social Security office in Toms River, New Jersey. Rosemary points out that there are various methods by which you can obtain a position with the Social Security Administration. You can take the Professional and Administrative Career Examination (P.A.C.E.). The results of this examination will help Social Security determine your qualifications. You can start out as a claims processing clerk or receptionist and by obtaining further experience and training be promoted to higher-level jobs such as data review technician or service representative. You can obtain experience in a Social Security office through a cooperative education or work-study program, which will allow you to obtain practical work experience while you attend college.

Is there any other way that you can learn whether you would like to work in a Social Security office? You might consider a job as a summer aide or part-time employee while attending high school. Janet Paz, a senior at Toms River South High School in Toms River, New Jersey, is employed as a summer aide in the Social Security office. Janet uses skills that she has learned in her high school business courses, such as data processing, mathematics, and typing, to perform her clerical duties. Some of her duties include preparing information concerning direct deposit of Social Security checks and asking questions concerning the status of someone's Social Security account. Janet communicates directly by computer with the national headquarters of the Social Security Administration in Baltimore, Maryland, while doing her work. At the age of seventeen, Janet is becoming familiar with Social Security procedures.

## VETERANS ADMINISTRATION

Another government agency that cares for a large number of older adults in its medical centers and outpatient clinics is the Veterans Administration. The VA operates 172 medical centers in every state of the union except Alaska and Hawaii. It has approximately 200,000 full-time employees and 30,000 part-time employees. About 90 percent of VA employees are associated with medical care for veterans. This includes more than 11,200 doctors and 31,500 nurses. In addition, the VA employs more than 30,700 licensed practical nurses and nursing assistants, 14,900 food service workers, and thousands of therapists, psychologists, dietitians, and other specialists to serve VA patients.

The Veterans Administration has as its primary function to provide assistance and care for veterans of all wars, including the Vietnam War. More than 15 million Americans served during World WarII (1941–45). It is now forty years since that war, and many of those veterans are sixty years old or older. Korean War veterans (1950–53) are also becoming older, and more of them are entering Veterans Administration hospitals.

The VA has other types of facilities besides medical centers for veterans in need of long-term care. Among these other facilities are domiciliaries, extended-care facilities such as the St. Albans VA Extended Care Center in New York.

In a modern health care system, health is not viewed merely as freedom from disease but as the capacity of the individual to function within his social environment, which includes the hospital. In VA medical centers it is the function of social work service to help patients and their families deal constructively with the interpersonal and environmental problems caused by or causing illness. Those problems, if left unresolved, can retard a patient's recovery or return to the community.

Social work treatment is particularly directed to the needs of persons confronted with crisis, life-threatening illnesses, traumatic losses, and chronic diseases or disabilities that require life-style changes and special living arrangements. The form of treatment may consist of individual, group, and family psychotherapy, financial and vocational counseling, and developing and utilizing community resources to promote appropriate discharge and after-care planning.

What sort of person does the Veterans Administration hire? The VA expects its employees to be highly trained and skilled in their profession. Whether they are nurses, social workers, psychologists, or therapists, they should enjoy working with older people. For a young person, it would be helpful if he had a close relationship with his grandparents or other significant older persons in his life. A young person coming from an extended family (three generations living in one home) would also have more experience in living and working with older adults.

If you are interested in Federal government employment and are accepted for employment in a VA facility, you will work in the largest hospital system in the country. You will also work in one of the finest health care systems in the world. The VA has been a pioneer in keeping health care personnel informed of the latest techniques used in medicine. New techniques are constantly being used in VA hospitals for helping older veterans. Recently two VA scientists, Rosalyn Yallow and Andrew Schally, were awarded the Nobel Prize for their studies of the endocrine system in the human body. All of these activities demonstrate the high level of research and medical care that is provided by the Veterans Administration to veterans of all wars.

## STATE GOVERNMENT

There are many jobs on the state level that include providing services and programs for older adults. Usually these jobs are found in the Department of Social Services of each state. Under this department, there is often a separate Division on Aging. The Department of Health has units that monitor the health maintenance of older adults. In many states the Department of Health has medical review teams that deal with the inspection and evaluation of hospitals, nursing homes, and other health facilities that serve older adults.

Jobs on the state level are usually civil service positions that require extensive education and training. As part of a state medical review team, you may be a doctor, a nurse, a dietitian, a pharmacist, a physical therapist, or other professional person. If you were a dietitian employed by the state, you might be assigned to inspect and evaluate a nursing home to determine if food is well prepared and food service properly supervised. You might check on the special diets that are prepared for older persons in the facility. In some cases you might discuss good nutrition practices with the food service personnel in the facilities that you visit. If you were a pharmacist, you might be employed by the state to check the kinds and dosage of medication prescribed for patients and determine if these drugs are in fact being distributed to older adult patients.

If the facility is found to be below required state standards, the state can recommend that admission of older adults be suspended or not allowed until conditions are improved. Normally, you would follow up on instructions provided by the patient's doctor. But the work that you do as a Department of Health employee would often determine if a patient is being treated correctly.

In all states, review of medical facilities is a continuous process. Various organizations are involved in this task. Most states have a Medicaid program, which is a medical assistance program for persons with low income. Some Medicaid employees provide information and referral services to older adults who request information about health care programs. Others serve as professionals who work with health care facilities.

Judy Eggers is a public health nurse who works for the state of New Jersey in the Medicaid program. Her job title is regional staff nurse. Judy visits nursing homes and checks on the level of nursing care in each facility in accordance with Medicaid regulations. She reviews medical records and interviews patients and staff. As a part of her duties, Judy visits homes and counsels families with regard to placing older adult members in nursing homes or other health care facilities. As part of a health care team, she helps determine the kind and level of care for older adults. In order to carry out her responsibilities, Judy must have a good knowledge of community resources.

When an older adult applies for or is in need of medical assistance, Judy is involved in coordinating the services of other health care professionals such as a physical therapist, an occupational therapist, a home health aide, a meals on wheels program, a retired senior volunteer program, and a senior companion program. One of her primary tasks is to identify community resources and help recommend a care plan to enable an older adult to remain in the community.

Judy has a varied and comprehensive background. She has almost twenty years of experience as a public health nurse in California and New Jersey. She has a BS degree in nursing from Cornell University in New York and is currently enrolled in a master's degree program in community health at Rutgers University in New Brunswick, New Jersey.

Suppose you wanted to become a nurse working for the Department of Health or as part of a state medical review team. What would be the advantages and disadvantages of working for the state? Obviously you would be expected to have experience and training in your profession. Most nurses employed by the state have five to ten years' experience in a hospital or acute care facility. As a representative of the state, you would be helping to advise and counsel other nurses in the facilities that you visit. At times you can advise staff members and discuss improved methods of assisting patients. The experience gained as a public health nurse can qualify you to become a consultant or nurse practitioner in the area of public health. You can also work for a large city or a county as a health care supervisor. Since you are a civil service employee, you will work a five-day week with holidays and weekends free. This is an advantage if you are used to working in a hospital.

What are the disadvantages? Some nurses would say that it is not terribly exciting to work with older adults. Certainly it will not be as exciting as being employed as a nurse in a general hospital, where you might be called to work in the emergency room with all types of patients. If your work includes visiting nursing homes, it may be depressing. The average age for nursing home residents is over eighty, and many are confused or resigned to death. You may become irritated by the way some patients are treated. This may occur because the staff personnel is poorly trained. Not all nurse's aides or other staff personnel in nursing homes are highly trained.

One other disadvantage of being a state health care employee is the travel. If your responsibilities include visiting health care facilities, you will be required to travel from one to another in all traffic conditions and in all weather. All of these factors should be kept in mind before you decide on a career in state government.

## OMBUDSMAN FOR THE INSTITUTIONALIZED ELDERLY

Most of us think that state employees who monitor conditions in nursing homes or other long-term care institutions are doctors, nurses, pharmacists, dietitians, or social workers. Recently, however, because of amendments to the Older Americans Act of 1965, persons with investigative or law enforcement experience are also needed. Many states, including Connecticut, Florida, Georgia, Massachusetts, New York, and New Jersey, have set up an Ombudsman's Office, which receives and investigates complaints relating to deficiencies in the health, welfare, and dignity of elderly persons living in institutional surroundings.

In New Jersey, the Office of the Ombudsman for the Institutionalized Elderly, which is headed by John Fay, has been given wide powers to determine if abuses have occurred against older adult residents of nursing homes, boarding homes, or other long-term care institutions. Although the office cannot prosecute, it can investigate and determine if the rights of an elderly person are being violated. Complaints come to the Office of the Ombudsman from victims, from outside community organizations, from employees, and from social workers who visit the nursing home or other health care facility.

Perhaps what makes an ombudsman program different from

other state agencies is that it also is mandated to investigate practices of state and county regulatory agencies, to insure that such agencies are fulfilling their responsibilities with regard to services afforded the institutionalized elderly.

If you were an employee of a state ombudsman program, what would be your duties and responsibilities? You must have investigative experience and be able to conduct interrogations. You need to be persistent in asking questions and obtaining answers concerning the rights of older adult patients. Yet you must be patient, as most victims experience difficulty in expressing themselves. You should have a knowledge of state laws that apply to older adults and of Medicare and Medicaid health insurance laws. In some cases, you might have to make recommendations against state agencies or public officials or suggest permanent changes in procedures or regulations to improve conditions for elderly patients.

Tom McNiff is an investigator for the New Jersey State Ombudsman for the Institutionalized Elderly who has over thirty years' experience in law enforcement. He works as part of a team to investigate complaints received by the Ombudsman's Office. Normally, Tom and a registered nurse investigator are sent to check conditions in a facility when a complaint is received. Staff requirements for these positions are five to ten years' experience as a registered nurse preferably in public health nursing, and for an investigator, five years' law enforcement experience with at least an associate in arts degree. Tom's job is important. By following up on complaints received by the Ombudsman's Office, he and other staff members help maintain high standards of care for older adults who reside in nursing homes or other institutions in New Jersey.

## STATE DIVISION ON AGING

The title for entry-level positions in the field of aging varies from state to state. Normally the requirements include one year of experience and a bachelor's degree. In one state there are career trainee positions that enable the college graduate to move from agency to agency. If he decides on a career in aging, he will remain in this office. Other states use the term field representative to designate the entry-level position in the aging field. Pennsylvania emphasizes advocacy in working with older adults; it has a position called aging advocate, which requires two years' experience as an advocate in the field of aging and a bachelor's degree. In New Jersey the entry-level position is called program development specialist.

Warren McClain is a program development specialist with the New Jersey Division on Aging. Warren is a generalist, able to move from one section or department to another and fulfill the responsibilities of whatever unit to which he is assigned. At present, Warren serves as coordinator and field representative to Area Agencies on Aging throughout the state. He contacts the Area Agencies and insures that the state office is kept up to date on requests and information that they may need.

Warren has worked at various jobs since coming to the division. He spent one year visiting nutrition sites as a field representative for the congregate nutrition program. For three years he worked as a housing specialist, concerned with program development. He helped provide information to community groups interested in developing housing for older adults. He also provided information regarding various housing alternatives for older adults who were considering or planning a change in living arrangements. This information included public housing projects, low-income housing, retirement villages, and continuing care and life care communities.

Warren acted as a resource person on housing alternatives for preretirement training for state employees and for various unions. He also was involved in a model housing project that developed programs for selected senior housing projects in the state. The program, called congregate housing, included provision of meals, housekeeping services, and personal services for frail elderly residents.

Warren has over seven years' experience working for the State of New Jersey. In 1974 he obtained a position with the New Jersey

State Department of Public Welfare in the food stamp program. Part of his job consisted of auditing food stamp cases and insuring that clients were receiving food stamps according to Federal regulations. In this job he visited the homes of clients, many of whom were older adults, and he found that he enjoyed talking with them, sharing their pictures of family and friends, and hearing about their life experiences. As a result, when he saw an opening in the *Civil Service Bulletin* in the field of aging, he applied for the position, and when accepted, transferred to the Division on Aging.

Warren enjoys working for the Division. He believes that you can have an impact on a large number of older adults when you work on the state level. You are aware of how Federal money is being spent for the various programs to help older adults. Of course, you don't work directly with older people as service providers do on the local level, but Warren does not see that as a major disadvantage. He says, "You'll never get rich working for the state, but it is fairly secure. In many cases you have the freedom to develop programs. It's fun to create. Of course that will depend upon your ability to take initiative, and it will also depend on your boss and how structured or unstructured he makes your job."

Warren graduated from Stockton State College in Pomona, New Jersey, in 1975 with a bachelor's degree in political science. He believes that political science is a good major for state employees because you are continually dealing with various levels of government in your job. At present he is enrolled in the master's program in gerontology at the University of Pennsylvania in Philadelphia. Warren is thirty years old, married, with two children.

## COUNTY GOVERNMENT

County government is where the vast majority of jobs in human service occur. In most county government jobs, you are dealing with the public at all age levels, not only older adults. However, there is no better level of government at which to gain experience and to find job openings. The reason for this is obvious. There is a high turnover of personnel in most county agencies, and the requirements and experience necessary may be less rigid than at the state or Federal level.

How do you get to be a human service employee who deals with a large number of older adults? Eileen Yost graduated with a BS degree in social work from Western Michigan University in 1971. Following graduation she returned to Lakewood, New Jersey, her hometown, and decided on a career in social service. Her father advised her to take any job in the field and gain experience. For her first job, she was over-qualified in education, but she took a position as income maintenance technician for the Ocean County Board of Social Services, in Toms River. Later she worked as a social worker for the organization for two years. In 1976 she saw an opening for supervisor of income technicians; she took the civil service test for the position and passed it. From 1976 she has been Supervisor of Income Maintenance Technicians.

Her unit takes applications for and processes food stamp applications. The guidelines for the food stamp program come from the U.S. Department of Agriculture in Washington, DC, but the states administer the program. How do older adults qualify for food stamps? The income limit varies depending on the net food stamp income of the individual. This is determined by deductions that are allowed for shelter, medical expenses, and other expenses. The income maintenance technician supervisor must review the application to determine whether the applicant qualifies for food stamp assistance.

As Eileen points out, there is a large population of older adults in Ocean County, and programs for them are expanding. Sometimes elderly people who come to the office to apply for food stamps are referred to other services, such as the crisis intervention center, which helps older adults who have recently been discharged from a hospital or are without a place to live because of fire or vandalism.

Your duties will be similar each day as an income maintenance technician. You will be expected to explain the food stamp program to each applicant and take applications. You will be required to follow guidelines that have been set by law. Sometimes you may be cynical because a person who applies for food stamps makes false statements concerning income. However, documentation is being increased each year to prevent fraud, and all applications must be processed in terms of law and regulations.

What sort of training will help you in performing your job as an income maintenance technician? Psychology courses or human relations courses will help you in public contact work. Eileen advises that you should go to college first, but some of the educational requirements may be waived if you have experience. If you want to advance in civil service positions, you will require further education if you start without a bachelor's degree. The position in the food stamp unit is only one of many human services positions on the county level. You may decide that you have the education and training for other jobs that will provide you with experience in the human services field and could lead to further specialization where you work primarily with older adults.

## PARKS AND RECREATION JOBS

Many counties throughout the United States have a Department of Parks and Recreation, and a large number of these are expanding services and programs. These programs include employees who work with older adults as activity directors and also recreation therapists who plan programs for the handicapped elderly.

Karen Mason is a recreation specialist for the Monmouth County Parks System in Lincroft, New Jersey. Her job is planning programs for special populations, including older adults. One of Karen's responsibilities is to describe the activities of the county park system when she visits senior centers and clubs throughout the county. She also discusses coming events in the county park system each week over radio station WHTG in Eatontown, New Jersey.

Karen helps older adults make use of county park facilities and enjoy plant and animal life within the county. She has taken older adults on one-day fishing trips to various parts of New Jersey and journeyed by bus to Cape Cod for some whale watching with a group of seniors. Sometimes Karen plans programs to meet the requirements of handicapped seniors, such as pottery classes for arthritic seniors. She finds her job varied and challenging.

Karen graduated from Brookdale Community College with an associate in arts degree in 1976 and then continued at Trenton State College, majoring in recreation and graduating with a BA in art therapy in 1979. Karen was involved in a cooperative education program as part of her college course, working at the Long Branch recreation department. Learning of an opening at the Long Branch Senior Center, she became supervisor of the center for a year. During this time she supervised programs at the center and handled special events concerned with the center for the city of Long Branch. Her activities included performing outreach to help make more seniors aware of programs at the center, providing arts and crafts programs, and bringing speakers to the center. Karen also worked with the Monmouth County Arts Council to bring artists to the center to teach painting, sculpture, and other art forms.

Karen's background is unusual. Widowed at twenty-three when her husband was killed in a motorcycle accident, Karen started at the local community college the following year. As she points out, "School helped me determine what I wanted to do and helped me get involved." Karen was able to combine two of her interests, art and human services, in her college major of art therapy. She has been able to utilize her college training in her jobs at a senior center and with a county park system.

## SALARIES IN GOVERNMENT POSITIONS

Starting salaries for Federal government employees are set by Congress and are a matter of public record. The following is a list of entrance salaries at each General Service level as of October 1980. Each grade level has ten steps and increases $3,000 to 4,000 from step one to step ten.

| | | | | |
|---|---|---|---|---|
| GS- 1 | $ 7,960 | | GS- 9 | $18,585 |
| GS- 2 | $ 8,951 | | GS-10 | $20,467 |
| GS- 3 | $ 9,766 | | GS-11 | $22,486 |
| GS- 4 | $10,963 | | GS-12 | $26,951 |
| GS- 5 | $12,266 | | GS-13 | $32,048 |
| GS- 6 | $13,672 | | GS-14 | $37,871 |
| GS- 7 | $15,193 | | GS-15 | $44,547 |
| GS- 8 | $16,826 | | GS-16 | $49,198 |

For Social Security Administration positions, a service representative would be hired at the GS-4 level and could rise to GS-7. A claims representative is normally hired at the GS-5 level and rises to GS-10. An operations supervisor in a Social Security office is employed at GS-10 or GS-11. For Veterans Administration employees, the starting salary depends on education and experience. A nurse with a bachelor's degree in nursing and a social worker with a master's in social work would start at the GS-9 level. A psychologist employed by the Veterans Administration would start at GS-12 or GS-13 level. Medical doctors are employed at the GS-14 level. If they are board certified and have specialized in some area of medicine, they are employed at the GS-16 level by the Veterans Administration.

Each state sets salary levels and administers civil service tests. In many instances a registered nurse, pharmacist, or other professional is not required to take a civil service exam but may provide evidence of education and training in order to be hired for a state position.

Entry-level salaries for civil service positions at state level range from $12,000 to $15,000. Experienced health care personnel can make over $20,000 in many states. An advantage of working in civil service positions is that you can rise rapidly in salary if you are promoted. This is also true of specialized skills that are in demand. Obviously a computer programmer in any state would have to be hired at a relatively high salary to compete with private industry.

Each county sets its own salary guide, and large urban counties pay higher salaries than rural counties. In Ocean County, New Jersey, an income maintenance aide, an employee taking applications for food stamps, earns between $6,000 and $8,000. With a college degree, an income maintenance specialist would earn between $12,000 and $16,000. A recreation supervisor in a county park system earns between $11,000 and $14,000. Overall, county salaries are lower than state or Federal, but you will be able to gain critical and necessary experience at this level.

Across the country you will not become affluent in human service jobs. Without college you will earn no more than $8,000 to $10,000. If you have a college degree, you probably will be employed at a salary between $10,000 and $15,000. You will be paid slightly higher if your degree is in demand, such as accounting, pharmacy, or dietetics. With a master's degree and with minimum experience you can start at the Federal level at $18,000. County and state levels will vary depending on the cost of living. You will be hired at a higher salary in Alaska, Hawaii, and other states where incomes and state resources are relatively high.

# Chapter XI

# Housing Alternatives

Perhaps you would like to work with older adults in the places where they live. These places vary tremendously in size and location and have been built for older adults in many states. Some states such as Florida and Arizona have a large number of older adults living in retirement communities.

In general, the main housing alternatives for older adults are retirement communities, senior citizen apartment buildings, homes for the elderly, and continuous care facilities. There are various reasons why older adults decide to move to a facility or location where most of the residents are of their age. Often the house where they have lived most of their life is too large since their family is grown up. Second, the high costs of energy or fuel associated with a large house may be an economic reason for moving. Third, taxes and maintenance of a thirty-, forty-, or fifty-year-old house may be a reason to move.

Retirement communities are popular with older adults because maintenance of grounds and buildings is included in monthly charges. Other services include recreational areas, common transportation, and police service. Senior citizen apartments are in demand for older adults who live in cities and urban areas. Some apartment buildings are subsidized by Federal or state government and require only a minimal rental for low-income older adults. Still other apartments provide services and specialized programs for handicapped or frail elderly residents. These services include cleaning, transportation, shopping, and other support services. Continual care facilities are similar to senior citizen apartments but also provide comprehensive medical facilities and nursing-home facilities for residents. There are also homes for older adults that have separate apartments or rooms and common facilities including cafeteria service.

Jobs in older adult housing include building manager, building superintendent, retirement village manager, and program or recreation director in a retirement community or other facility. Often professional personnel have elected to live and work in a retirement community or near a senior citizen apartment complex. These include doctors, nurses, social workers, and various types of therapists.

*FRIENDSET*

An example of an apartment complex for older adults is Friendset, in the Coney Island section of Brooklyn, New York. There are 258 apartments in this building in which 320 older adults live. Most apartments have one resident, but a number of couples reside in the building.

Ann Neiland is Housing Manager at Friendset. She deals with day-to-day concerns and problems of the residents, many of which concern personal finances. Some of the residents have difficulty in reading or writing, and some are foreign-born and do not speak or write English. Sometimes Ann must find a translator who can speak Russian or Yiddish to communicate with residents concerning bills or other financial matters. She must also deal with relatives and others who attempt to contact building residents.

How did Ann get the experience that enables her to carry out her responsibilities as manager? Her sociology professor at Bridgewater State College in Bridgeton, Massachusetts, encouraged students to become involved in community projects. Ann chose as her field work the project of working with older adults, and she succeeded in starting a transportation program and shuttle bus service. When she graduated with a degree in sociology in 1973, she obtained a job as activities director in a nursing home, where she planned programs for residents. She started classes and encouraged residents to write and direct their own plays. In 1975 Ann decided to go to New York and seek employment in the field of aging. She did not know anyone in New York, but through the telephone directory she contacted various agencies and got a job. Her first job was at a nutrition site for older adults in an Episcopal church in Brooklyn. Later she worked for the meals on wheels component of the nutrition program and became director of the program. In May 1979 Ann applied for and obtained the position of housing manager at Friendset. Ann is employed by JASA, a Jewish community service organization that supervises the meals on wheels program and also the Friendset housing project.

Ann enjoys her job as housing manager. Her office is a hub of activity for over 300 older adults. She points out that a senior citizen housing manager must have a well-planned program. When seniors are busy and involved in various activities, they are contented. Frequent bus trips and other day trips are helpful by encouraging seniors to leave their apartment and socialize with their friends and thus to think less of their current aches and pains.

## *BUILDING SUPERINTENDENT*

At twenty-one, Ben Baez has a varied background to qualify for the position of building superintendent at Friendset. Ben supervises four porters, all of whom are older than himself. He urges them to continue their schooling and obtain further training, because they are high school dropouts like himself.

At sixteen Ben started working for his father, who is also a building superintendent in New York City. Although Ben dropped out of high school, he continued to attend night school. He studied electricity, carpentry, and boiler supervision. At eighteen he got a job as porter in an apartment complex, and six months later he became a handyman. Ben believes that working as a handyman in a building sharpens your skills. You must be able to meet residents and talk with them about their maintenance problems. Often you must enter the apartment of a resident and perform maintenance work. You must also work with other members of the staff. As a porter you need to have all the skills necessary to keep the building clean from top to bottom.

Ben also urges young people to join a building trades union. "In most cities there is a building trades union. Join the union and let them know you are interested in advancing. Most unions have a program of education and training. Every course completed will help you in your work."

What skills do you need to become a superintendent of a senior citizen apartment complex? You must be able to work with employees and with the managers or owners of the building. Ben enjoys working with the tenants. Often they invite him into their apartments. He listens to their problems, and if necessary he explains why he cannot handle a problem or request that they have made. Other skills needed include keeping up with the latest fire regulations, boiler regulations, and other laws passed by the city and state regarding senior housing complexes.

*SOCIAL SERVICE COORDINATOR*

Today many senior citizen apartment complexes have a social worker or social service coordinator whose job it is to provide counseling and assistance to residents. Justine Klein is employed as a social service coordinator at Asbury Towers in Asbury Park, New Jersey. Asbury Towers is a senior citizen high-rise apartment building supervised by the Presbyterian Homes of New Jersey. Justine's main tasks are helping residents to fill out forms and arranging homemaker services for frail or ill residents. Often she must contact agencies such as Social Security and Medicaid to obtain information. At other times she arranges transportation for tenants who need to go shopping or to a doctor or other professional in town.

Justine's background includes a bachelor's degree in psychology from Russell Sage College in Troy, New York. Before going to Asbury Towers, Justine had extensive experience working with older adults as an occupational therapist in Marlboro Psychiatric Hospital in Marlboro, New Jersey, and as a coordinator of transportation services for older adults for the Monmouth County Social Services Board.

## FOOD SERVICE MANAGER

Another type of service provided in senior citizen apartment complexes is food service. This may be a nutrition program or a cafeteria that provides meals for residents. Bill Burroughs is Food Service Manager at Francis Asbury Manor in Ocean Grove, New Jersey. Bill is employed by Weyland Food Services, a company that provides food services for many health care facilities and senior residences throughout New Jersey and Pennsylvania. Francis Asbury Manor is operated by the United Methodist Homes of New Jersey and has 280 residents. Food service provides about 300 servings at each meal or about 1,000 meals per day. About 30 mobile meals are sent to various parts of Ocean Grove every day.

According to Bill Burroughs, one of the main factors in the job of a food service manager is cost control in buying foods. At twenty-seven, Bill is responsible for a yearly budget of $750,000. Since Bill is accountable for the budget, he must decide what foods to buy and determine the time to buy at the lowest prices. Invariably, the highest cost item is meat. By preparing a weekly cost report, Bill watches food prices carefully during the year and attempts to buy when prices are lowest. He also develops a cost inventory of items such as meat, frozen and fresh vegetables, milk and ice cream, paper goods, and soap. Bill is in day-to-day contact with his cooks and encourages them to conserve and not be wasteful in preparing food.

The second major factor in the job is getting to know the food tastes of residents. After lunch is served, Bill can usually be found chatting with residents and attempting to find out their likes and dislikes in food. Sometimes it is a matter of educating residents to institutional cooking, that is, why food is not seasoned with salt and why it must be cooked in a certain manner. Bill also works closely with a consulting dietitian who helps in planning menus and providing dietary information and counseling to residents.

The Weyland company expects employees to find out what their residents like or dislike. Therefore, a survey is taken once a year. This survey includes questions on food, appetizers, service, and food for holidays or special events. From these surveys, Bill often tries new methods of serving. One experiment was to have a holiday buffet instead of the usual cafeteria service.

Bill tries to be honest when talking about food service with older adults. Sometimes he admits, "We blew it today." He admits that his staff isn't perfect. There will always be complaints about food and food service. But he emphasizes to older adults, "Didn't you make mistakes when you cooked for your husband?" Through continued feedback, the residents come to know Bill and defend him from a new resident who doesn't seem to like anything that is prepared in the kitchen.

What are the disadvantages of Bill's job? Obviously people will always complain about the food. Sometimes the food service manager will have to ignore complaints and other times check out complaints to find out what is wrong. As far as labor is concerned, food service managers find it difficult to motivate their employees, who are unskilled and do not make very high salaries. Many high school students are also employed in food service facilities; that means a high turnover of labor because they usually work two years and then go to college or other employment.

And there is weekend work. Bill's company expects supervisors to work every other weekend. Sometimes Bill takes the night supervisor's place to meet and work with the employees on the evening shift.

What training do you need to become a food service manager in a senior citizen housing facility? First, you must be in good health. Kitchen work is demanding, and you will be involved in lifting and moving of pots, pans, and kitchen equipment. You can expect to receive on-the-job training. Most food service managers start in the kitchen and work up to higher-paying supervisory positions. Bill started in high school and continued to work part time in college as a cook at the Navesink House, a senior citizen housing facility in Red Bank, New Jersey

When Bill received his degree in history and government from Monmouth College, he hoped for a career in government. There was a freeze on hiring at that time, however, so he continued to work as a cook at Navesink House. In 1976 the business manager of Navesink House decided to bring in an outside agency to provide food service, and Bill was hired by the Weyland Food Service company as Assistant Manager. After eight months he became Manager of Food Services at Navesink House, and in January 1980 he moved to Francis Asbury Manor as Food Service Manager.

Bill believes strongly in obtaining further education while you are performing your job. Accounting and food service management courses mean a lot more to you when you are actually doing the work. To be certified as a food service manager, you must have taken a 90-hour course under the direction of a registered dietitian. Courses are also offered at community colleges and universities in which you can study food service management.

## RETIREMENT VILLAGE EMPLOYMENT

As previously indicated, retirement villages are located throughout the United States. In most cases, the only restrictions are on the age of the resident (55 or over) and the age of children who live with residents. Retirement communities usually range from 1,000 to 1,500 units and 2,000 to 4,000 residents. Although there is much volunteer work in these communities in home care, nursing care, maintenance, transportation, and village government, there is still need for paid employees.

Since the residents vary widely in age and background, it is important to plan different activities for different age groups. Activities that are usually carried out in a community room or recreation hall include educational courses on topics such as business, current events, foreign languages, or travel. Other activities include sports clubs concerned with bowling, fishing, hunting, shuffleboard, swimming, and many others. Arts and crafts activities include painting, sculpture, and jewelry making.

Lily Stauch, Recreation Director of Leisure Village West in Lakehurst, New Jersey, is kept busy planning and developing activities for over 3,000 residents. In the recreation clubhouse and throughout the village, over forty clubs participate in many different kinds of activities and programs.

What suggestions does Lily offer to someone who wants to become a program director for a retirement community? "You must be people-oriented. You must be a leader and organizer who can relate to any age group. Obviously you must like and respect older adults. But at the same time you must have strength in your own beliefs. Retirement community residents need direction and want to have confidence in your ability to carry out decisions and plan programs for them."

According to Lily, you must start early to work in jobs in which you relate to people. Gain experience in working with any age group. Obtaining an education as a recreation leader is fine, but the ability to be a recreation director comes from experience. And don't wait till you graduate; work in the summer or during the college term to get experience in recreation. Lily has been planning programs for older adults for nine years.

How did Lily become a recreation director? Her mother had a catering business that sometimes planned parties for retirement community residents. Lily helped out on weekends while working in a bank. She became particularly good at planning parties and programs for residents of retirement communities including Leisure

Village East. Soon the management asked her to work full time doing exactly that.

All of the jobs mentioned in this chapter are interesting and challenging. What kind of salaries do these persons earn? Building managers earn from $15,000 to $25,000. Very large apartment complex managers may earn $35,000. Building superintendents receive benefits by living in the facility, and their cash salary is somewhat lower. Salaries also depend on prevailing union wages if they are members of a union. Salaries for social service coordinators vary depending on whether the person is a graduate social worker. If not, the salaries would be between $10,000 and $15,000. Salaries for food service managers range from $12,000 to $20,000. In a large facility you might earn $25,000 or more. Recreation directors start at $10,000 and range in salary up to $18,000 in large retirement communities.

# Chapter XII

# Organizations and Agencies in the Field of Aging

You should be familiar with the national organizations and agencies that are active in the field of aging. These organizations are involved in planning and developing public policy, participating in legislative hearings before congressional committees, and providing information to members of their organizations on issues affecting the lives of older adults.

In the national capital, congressional committees include the Select Committee on Aging of the House of Representatives and the Special Committee on Aging of the Senate, which deal with legislation concerning older adults. In addition there are many city, county, and state organizations located in Washington that are involved in obtaining a better life for everyone in their later years. Education associations including the American Association of Community and Junior Colleges, the International Center for Social Gerontology, and national and regional gerontology associations are involved in the aging field. All of these organizations conduct special projects, studies, and research that often lead to public policy change and a better life for older adults.

The national organizations have a great impact on aging policy through their publications, newsletters, and information distributed to their members throughout the country. The main national organizations in the field of aging are the National Council on Aging, the National Council of Senior Citizens, and the

American Association of Retired Persons, all in Washington, DC. Other organizations involved in developing and advocating better policies and programs for older adults include the Gray Panthers, in Philadelphia.

For over thirty years the National Council on Aging has been involved in promoting and developing improved programs and services for older adults. It works with and through other organizations to develop a nationwide concern for older persons. It also is involved in designing methods and identifying resources to meet these needs. It serves as a central and national resource for planning, training, and consultation. Its major programs include the National Institute of Senior Centers, the National Institute of Adult Day Care, the National Voluntary Organizations for Independent Living for the Aging, the National Center on Arts and the Aging, and many others.

The National Council on Aging also administers demonstration projects that employ, train, and utilize older persons in different ways. One of its projects is the Senior Community Service Project (SCSP). The major objective of the SCSP is providing additional income and community involvement for elderly, low-income persons. It meets this objective by establishing part-time community service work experience and training for older adults. Funds for the program are provided by the U.S. Department of Labor. The program, which was started in 1968 in a few communities, has expanded until it provides employment for thousands of older adults throughout the country. All of the other national organizations concerned with older adults participate in this project.

A local sponsor that works with the National Council to provide part-time employment for older adults is United Progress, Inc., a community action program in Trenton, New Jersey. United Progress, Inc. has developed a work-supervised program in which older adults fifty-five and over are provided with part-time employment and learn new skills. These older adults are employed in public and private agencies throughout Mercer County.

Sue Ricciardi is a senior program coordinator for United Progress, Inc. At twenty-six Sue has over four years' experience in the field of employment counseling for older adults. She finds her job challenging and rewarding. She is involved in counseling, job development, organizing activities, and providing training for older adults. She supervises a staff of four whose primary task is contacting employers at the worksites scattered throughout Mercer County and monitoring work attendance of older adults.

Sue received her experience for this position as a volunteer and through education and internship. Sue worked as a camp counselor while in high school. She also performed volunteer work in a local hospital and a nursing home. After high school Sue entered Upsala College in East Orange, New Jersey, and majored in sociology. She transferred to Adelphi University in Garden City, New York, in her junior year and graduated in 1977 with a bachelor's degree in social work. While at Adelphi, Sue participated in student internships, which consisted of supervised work programs that enabled her to obtain firsthand experience. One internship involved leading discussion groups for older adults at Samuel Field YM-YWHA on topics such as current events, issues concerning older adults, and community services for older adults.

Upon returning to New Jersey in the summer of 1977, Sue obtained a temporary position with United Progress, Inc., which involved recruiting for Head Start, another community agency program. In September 1977 Sue was hired as a full-time employee by United Progress, Inc. Her duties included testing individuals for job attitudes before they entered job training at the agency to insure that they had some background and interest for the program. Through this experience Sue learned about other community agencies in the Trenton and Mercer County area. In April 1978 she became director of the program, supervising placement of fifty older adults and fifty adult work experience employees. As the older adult section of the program continued to expand, Sue was placed in complete charge of that program, which expanded to over 110 enrollees by 1980 and is continuing to expand.

Sue comments, "To gain experience for this type of job, you can work with seniors in some activity or obtain a job in an employment agency or personnel department to learn about job placement or job training. Since you will be contacting community agencies for placement of older adults, you must be aware of the agencies that are active in your area."

According to Sue, "You must be convinced yourself that older adults are conscientious workers. You must be determined to sell employers on the idea of hiring older adults. You must have patience in working with older adults. Many times you have to place yourself in their situation. If you provide them with the skills they need to succeed, they will gain confidence in themselves."

Sue doesn't feel there are many disadvantages in her job. There isn't time to do everything she would like to do. There is the problem of budget and finances. Many social agencies work on a yearly budget that can be cut through changes in the amount of funds provided by the Federal government. Nevertheless, she believes her position as director of employment has given her the opportunity to develop many different skills.

For persons who want to enter the employment field for older adults, Sue suggests that they obtain a B.A. degree in sociology or social work. Volunteer work in community agencies, particularly with active healthy older adults, would be helpful. As you gain experience, you may also develop contacts that can help you in getting a job. Sue has eight Hispanic older adults enrolled in her program, and she believes that a knowledge of languages is important—particularly the language of the largest ethnic group in your area. Finally you must be willing to work with older adults in all types of situations.

The National Retired Teachers Association (NRTA) and the American Association of Retired Persons (AARP) are other national organizations dedicated to helping older Americans achieve retirement lives of independence and purpose. Both organizations were founded by Dr. Ethel Percy Andrus, a California educator for more than 40 years. With a combined membership of more than 12 million, the associations are the nation's largest organization of older Americans. National headquarters is in Washington, DC, and the membership division and Western office is in Long Beach, California.

The American Association of Retired Persons publishes *Modern Maturity,* a bimonthly magazine devoted to articles on older adult living. The organization is involved in legislative representation and has specialists in most states advocating the rights and concerns of older adults. Most of this representation is voluntary, and NRTA-AARP has state legislative committees in all fifty states.

Other national programs include a health education program, a 55/Alive Mature Driving program, a crime prevention program designed to help older adults avoid becoming crime victims, and a tax aide program that trains members to assist older persons in income tax return preparation. A Widowed Person Service provides community programs for recent widows. Intergenerational programs bring young and old together, and purchase privilege programs provide members with discounts at car rental companies and hotel/motel chains.

Other programs in AARP promote education for older adults such as the Institute of Lifetime Learning, and the Action for Independent Maturity (AIM), which provides preretirement information and counseling.

The National Council of Senior Citizens concentrates on pushing legislation and improving Federal regulations to generate much-needed services and increased security for older people. The organization came into existence twenty years ago as a result of a series of meetings during the White House Conference on Aging in 1961. The National Council of Senior Citizens was extremely active in securing the passage of Medicare, a program of Federal health insurance for older adults.

Since then the National Council has been involved in advocating and improving laws concerned with health care legislation, Social Security benefits, employment for older adults, transportation, and senior citizen housing. Nationally, it is one of the largest developers of senior citizen housing, with 15 projects built and under construction as of 1981.

Today the National Council of Senior Citizens is one of the largest organizations working in the field of aging. It has nearly four million members in 4,000 clubs throughout the United States. Although its primary purpose was improved health care for older adults, it has become involved in other key issues affecting older adults such as energy policy. Since 1978, when oil prices began rising at a rapid rate throughout the country, the National Council of Senior Citizens has worked with other organizations to persuade Congress to pass legislation providing fuel assistance for low-income people including older adults.

Project Energy Care was a nationwide effort to publicize the Low Income Energy Assistance program in 1980–81 by the National Council of Senior Citizens. The NCSC identified local sponsors in each state who were given the responsibility of providing outreach services and information concerning energy assistance programs for older adults.

One local sponsor in New Jersey was the Community Outreach Program for Senior Adults (COPSA), a unit of the Community Mental Health Center of Rutgers University Medical School in Piscataway, New Jersey. This organization was established to serve elderly persons, particularly those not in nursing homes but needing supportive services in order to remain in their home environment as long as possible. The program was begun because few elderly people were being served by mental health centers. Lack of knowledge about mental health and related social services, lack of transportation, poor physical health, and fear of the mental health centers prevented older adults from visiting the centers. COPSA was started to provide seniors with information on services available, enabling them to utilize these services, and advocating on their behalf so that they could remain in their communities in good mental health as long as possible.

Rick De Gironimo is Assistant Coordinator for COPSA. During

1980–81 he was a coordinator of Project Energy Care for the National Council of Senior Citizens. This project consisted of providing education to older adults about hypothermia (excessive loss of heat from the body due to cold) and hyperthermia (excessive heat in the summer that affects the body.) Because of the high cost of energy, older adults were turning down their heating systems in the winter and reducing the use of air conditioning in summer. The project also provided advocacy to seniors to aid them in obtaining benefits and entitlements concerned with the energy assistance program.

Rick and other members of the staff helped seniors obtain educational material on energy-related topics. Workshops were organized on energy assistance for groups of seniors throughout Middlesex County. Information and education concerning hypothermia and hyperthermia were provided for senior groups.

What sort of background and education help Rick carry out his job effectively? Rick was unsure what he wanted to do when he received his bachelor's degree in economics and sociology from Livingston College in New Brunswick, New Jersey, in 1976. However, he obtained employment with two county service agencies, first in a food stamp unit and next in an income maintenance unit. Thus he became involved in the field of social work.

In 1977 he enrolled in the Rutgers Graduate School of Social Work and decided to major in community organization and planning. Through his field placement experience as part of his academic coursework, he was assigned to work with tenant and community organizations in low-income apartments in the Perth Amboy area. He also became aware of the problems of older residents in these apartments and helped to identify and deliver services to them.

When Rick graduated from Rutgers in 1979 with a master's degree in social work, he had decided on a career in community organization and planning. The job market for social workers was not good that summer, but through persistence and application to many agencies and programs, he obtained a position with COPSA in December.

What advice does Rick have for recent graduates in social work? Rick says, "Don't sell yourself short. Be proud of what you know and can do. You are a human service planner. Social workers are able to do networking and organization coordinating. Social workers see the total picture of the client's needs and can link the client with the system. He or she can fill in the gaps that are needed for the client."

Although social workers are generalists in the field of human services, Rick feels that often they are at a disadvantage in dealing with other professionals. Sometimes it is difficult to get other professionals to treat social workers as equals. Nevertheless, Rick enjoys being assistant coordinator. He likes being an advocate for older adults and working with them on a one-to-one basis. He likes networking with other organizations, and he has picked up a lot of knowledge concerning older adults in two years with the agency.

The Senior Community Service Project directed by Sue Ricciardi, and Project Energy Care coordinated by Rick De Gironimo demonstrate that it is possible for young persons to work for a local sponsor of a national organization that administers nationwide programs or projects for older adults.

## EMPLOYMENT OPPORTUNITIES IN WASHINGTON, DC

Are there employment opportunities for high school or college graduates on the staffs of national organizations? The answer is a qualified yes. National headquarters positions are located primarily in Washington, DC. Competition for entry-level positions is keen. Yet each of the national organizations requires skilled personnel who are qualified in the field of aging.

Sometimes college graduates who go to Washington in search of employment start as support staff personnel because of lack of higher-level position openings. Support staff are in demand that possess good communication skills, type 60 words per minute, have a high school diploma or the equivalent, and have two years' experience in business or government.

In addition, professional staff personnel with training in social work, gerontology, adult education, and legislative representation are required. Journalism skills are in demand since all of the national organizations publish or distribute newsletters, pamphlets, and magazines. For example, the National Council on Aging publishes *Perspectives on Aging,* the American Association of Retired Persons publishes a monthly news bulletin, the National Council of Senior Citizens publishes *Senior Citizen News,* and the Gray Panthers publish the *Gray Panther Network.*

Betty Shepherd, a program associate for the National Council on Aging, uses her journalism and editing skills in her work. She is editor of two newsletters, one concerned with rural aging and one on adult day care. Other aspects of her job include contact with persons who are involved in the field of aging throughout the country and responding to inquiries from members of NCOA and other interested persons about programs and services.

What advice does Betty give to the student entering the field of aging? "Learning by experience is still the best method to become involved in aging. Try to work in a variety of programs. You cannot learn about program development in school. You will learn much more about programs and services talking to people who are in the field of aging." Perhaps you want to become employed in aging but you have majored in business administration and have management skills. No matter what your major, Betty urges that you obtain some training in gerontology either by summer study, semester study, or certificate training programs.

Prior to going to Washington, Betty was an elementary school teacher in Clinton, Iowa. After visiting her sister one summer, Betty decided to seek employment in the capital. On her second job interview, she obtained a secretarial position with the National Council on Aging.

There are disadvantages in working for a national organization. If you like providing direct services to older adults, then working for a national organization is not for you. You will not be a direct service provider. You will not be concerned primarily with activities that are taking place for older adults on a local or county level. Often you will be working nights and weekends on special projects, programs, or legislative hearings concerned with aging.

But there are many advantages. You will be part of a team. The staff of a national organization is committed to a cause—to enhance or improve the life of older adults. You will not be a part of a profit-oriented business firm, but instead employed by a non-profit agency. You will be looking at the total picture, the total system of programs and services for older adults. You will also be formulating and developing public policy to improve the status of all older adults, and you will be involved with people in the aging field from all over the country. Betty says that the part of her job she likes best is interacting with people. She finds that the direct service providers that she comes in contact with are truly committed to their work.

Thus you have to make this decision before you start your search for a career that will provide you with satisfaction and lifelong rewards. If you like working directly with older adults and providing direct services, you will be unhappy working at the state or Federal level or for a national organization. On the other hand, if you like to plan and participate in developing public policy, you may be able to qualify for an entry-level position in a national organization.

## SALARIES

Salaries depend on whether the agency is county, state, or Federal. On the national level, national organizations must be competitive with government and private agencies working in the field of aging.

An employment coordinator, depending upon the size of the project, earns between $12,000 and $18,000. A social worker earns between $15,000 and $25,000. The National Association of Social

Workers recently recommended the following salaries:

| | |
|---|---|
| Bachelor of Social Work | $15,220 |
| Graduate Social Worker—MSW | $18,990 |
| Certified Social Worker—ACSW | $21,980 |
| Social Work Fellow | $26,660 |

Some local, county, and state agencies cannot pay these salaries, but other states and localities with greater financial resources are meeting the recommendations.

On a national level, secretaries for national organizations start at $11,000 and move to $14,000. Since many college graduates move to large cities such as Washington, DC, there is much competition for entry-level positions. An entry-level specialist in aging earns about $14,000 to $15,000. A program specialist or education specialist or associate earns from $17,000 to $27,000. Salary is often determined by level of responsibility and accountability for projects in aging. Legislative specialists with legal training or wide experience in aging earn over $30,000. As in all industries, your responsibilities, experience, and training will determine your salary.

# Bibliography

Academy for Educational Development, *Never Too Old to Learn.* New York: Academy for Educational Development, 1974.

Atchley, Robert C. *The Social Forces in Later Life; An Introduction to Social Gerontology.* 2nd ed. Belmont, CA: Wadsworth Publishing Company, 1977.

Binstock, Robert H., ed. *Handbook of Aging and the Social Sciences.* New York: Van Nostrand Reinhold Company, 1977.

Birren, James E., and Schaie, K. Warner, eds. *Handbook of Psychology of Aging.* New York: Van Nostrand Reinhold Co., 1977.

Botwinick, J. *Aging and Behavior.* New York: Springer, 1973.

Boyd, Rosamonde, and Oakes, Charles. *Foundations of Practical Gerontology,* 2nd ed. rev. Columbia: University of South Carolina Press.

Butler, Robert N. *Why Survive? Being Old in America.* New York: Harper & Row, 1975.

Comfort, Alex, *A Good Age.* New York: Crown Publishers, Inc., 1976.

DeCrow, Roger. *New Learning for Older Americans: An Overview of the National Effort.* Washington, D.C.: Adult Education Association of the United States, 1975.

Gelfand, Donald E., and Olsen, Jody K. "Aging Network: Programs and Services." Volume VIII in Springer Series of Adulthood and Aging. New York, 1980.

Korim, Andrew. *Older Americans and Community Colleges: A Guide for Program Implementation.* Washington, D.C.: American Association of Community and Junior Colleges, 1974.

Kubler-Ross, Elizabeth. *Death: The Final Stage of Growth.* Englewood, N.J.: Prentice-Hall Inc., 1975.

Merrill, Toni. *Activities for the Aged and Infirm.* Springfield, Ill.: Charles Thomas, 1967.

Mitford, Jessica. *The American Way of Death,* New York: Crest Books, Fawcett World Library, 1963.

Pennsylvania State University, Gerontology Center, Institute for the Study of Human Development. *Basic Concepts in Aging.* University Park, 1976.

Rossman, Parker. *Hospice,* New York: Fawcett Columbine, 1979.

Rosenfeld, Albert. *Prolongevity.* New York: Alfred A. Knopf, 1976.

Saul, Shura. *Aging: An Album of People Growing Old.* New York: John Wiley & Sons, 1974.

Older Americans Act of 1965, As Amended. U.S. Department of Health, Education, and Welfare, Office of Human Development, Administration on Aging. DHEW Publication No. (OHD) 76-20170.

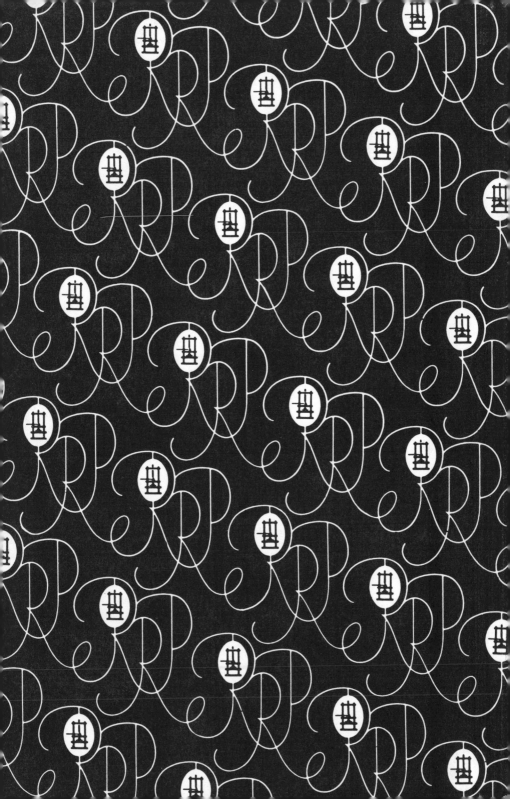